What leaders are saying about Scott Wilson and **IMPACT**:

"Scott was born for this! The 31 years he's been in pastoral ministry have been for this moment and this calling ... to help Lead Pastors become all God has called them to be. I can tell you right now that Scott is the greatest spiritual father in America. That's a fact."

—*John Maxwell, No. 1* New York Times *bestselling author, coach and speaker who has sold more than 24 million books in 50 languages*

"Very few people challenge me or encourage me like Scott Wilson. He is a pastor of pastors, a leader of leaders. You can't be around Scott very long without getting God ideas! If you're ready to grow—personally and organizationally—I can't imagine a better mentor or spiritual father."

—*Mark Batterson, Lead Pastor of National Community Church, Washington, D.C., and* New York Times *bestselling author*

"Leaders are learners. It is inherent in leaders to improve. So, in their quest to grow, they seek out the best. They look for people with fresh eyes—those who see what they don't see—so they can become their best. Biblically, this is played out by Jethro and Moses. Jethro saw what Moses didn't see. Scott Wilson is a modern-day Jethro. He has pastored, and he knows what it's like to live in the trenches. He's built a ministry that's esteemed and respected. If you're a pastor, borrow from Scott's vision. He'll help you *see* better, he'll help you *be* better, and he'll help you *become* better."

—*Gerald Brooks, D.D., D.C.L., Founding Pastor of Grace Outreach Center, Plano, Texas, Author of* Understanding Your Pain Threshold, What I Learned While Destroying a Church, *and* The Building Blocks of Leadership

"I doubt you've ever read a more unvarnished, transparent, and unfiltered leadership book than *Impact: Releasing the Power of Influence* by my long-time friend, Scott Wilson. When I read this book, I laughed, I cried, I hurt, I celebrated, I learned, and I grew. No doubt, you'll do the same. I recommend *Impact* not just to you—but to all the leaders in your life. You'll love it, but more than that, it will change you."

—*Sam Chand, leadership consultant and author of* Harnessing the Power of Tension

"Want to grow your church to 1,000 plus? If so, I am pleased to recommend Pastor Scott Wilson and his organization, Ready, Set, Grow. They will help you apply biblical principles and practical strategies that will result in fulfillment of Isaiah 54:2-3. So, get ready to enlarge the place of your tent, stretch out your curtains, lengthen your cords, and strengthen your stakes. You will expand!"

—*Walter Harvey, President, National Black Fellowship, Assemblies of God*

IMPACT

Releasing the Power of Influence

SCOTT WILSON

AVAIL

Cover design: Joe De Leon
Cover photo: Andrew van Tilborgh

ISBN: 978-1-954089-30-3   1 2 3 4 5 6 7 8 9 10

Printed in the United States of America

CONTENTS

IMPACT

Scott knows ministry can be like navigating a minefield. Revenue ceilings. Staffing problems. Management issues. Leadership misses. Systems dysfunction. Feeling trapped. Hit any one of those mines, and it could all be over. He's walked through that ministry minefield and gotten to the other side. Those obstacles are real, and there's real danger if you hit them. There is a way through, and I can show you.

Scott has over three decades of experience in growing top-tier leaders in ministry and the marketplace. He's helped thousands of senior leaders around the world blow the lid off their leadership caps, learn how to organize their personal lives for maximum impact, and set up duplicatable staffing/organizational systems for church growth. He has equipped hundreds of men and women around the world to succeed in everything from church planting to leading worldwide faith-based networks.

Scott has spent a lifetime building the best-in-class team of experts who have the ability to transform thinking, explode current capacity, and help deploy renewable systems for impacting your community, your family, your church, and your world. Scott's newest company, Ready Set Grow, is a hybrid of True North strategy, real-time, in-the-moment coaching, and duplicatable models that will catapult you into a way of living and leading that you always hoped was achievable. If you're in a place where you need a systematic process and hands-on coaching, the RSG team is here to help! Go to ReadySetGrowChurch.com to partner your church with our team of experts.

Part 1

Multiplied Impact

Chapter 1

EXPONENTIAL LEADERSHIP

A few years ago, several close friends started really getting into CrossFit. They were crazy about it, and several times, they invited me to join them. After hearing how excited they were about it, I told them, "Sure, count me in. It'll be fun." I soon discovered CrossFit wasn't just a gym, it was a cult. Okay, not really a cult, but it's a bunch of highly committed, fiercely determined, rabidly enthusiastic people. (Kind of sounds like a cult, doesn't it?) I met them at 3:30 p.m. for workouts that included the local CrossFit owner. One exhausting WOD (work out of the day) wasn't enough for these guys, so they did two. In case you haven't ever participated in CrossFit, here's a clue: They wear shirts that say, "Our warmups are harder than your workouts." Those first few months "in the box" were way more difficult than anything I had ever done.

At times as a leader, I felt a lot like I did after my first CrossFit workout—exhausted, confused, and wondering how long I could take it. Over the years, I've made more than my fair share of mistakes. In this book, I want to share some of the lessons I've learned—often the hard way—about the nature of leading people. My hope is that these lessons will have the opposite effect of my first workout with my friends ... that you'll be energized, with a clear and compelling vision, and eager to see what God has for you in the future. The principles apply to leaders in all fields: large-scale businesses, small businesses, nonprofits, and churches.

Forbes magazine is one of the most prestigious and respected leadership journals in the world. In an article on the top 100 quotes on leadership, we find some brilliant ones from the fields of business, government, the military, and sports:

- Jack Welch: "Before you are a leader, success is all about growing yourself. When you become a leader, success is all about growing others."
- John C. Maxwell: "A leader is one who knows the way, goes the way, and shows the way."
- Peter Drucker: "Leadership is lifting a person's vision to high sights, the raising of a person's performance to a higher standard, the building of a personality beyond its normal limitations."
- Brian Tracy: "Become the kind of leader that people would follow voluntarily; even if you had no title or position."
- Jim Rohn: "The challenge of leadership is to be strong, but not rude; be kind, but not weak; be bold, but not a bully; be

thoughtful, but not lazy; be humble, but not timid; be proud, but not arrogant; have humor, but without folly."

◆ Phil Jackson: "As a leader your job is to do everything in your power to create the perfect conditions for success by benching your ego and inspiring your team to play the game the right way. But at some point, you need to let go and turn yourself over to the basketball gods. The soul of success is surrendering to what is."

◆ Stephen Covey: "Effective leadership is putting first things first. Effective management is discipline, carrying it out."[1]

Some people read these quotes and instantly conclude, "That's what I'm talking about! That's the kind of leader I want to be!" But others aren't so sure. Maybe they've tried to lead and got burned by criticism, and they've scaled their vision to a lower level to reduce the blowback. Maybe they've lived in the shadow of a remarkable leader, and they can't imagine having a comparable impact. Maybe they've just never seen themselves as dynamic, visionary leaders.

After working with literally thousands of people over the last 30 years, I've come to the unshakable conclusion that everyone can raise the level of their influence. It's possible, it's within reach, but first, we need to take a cold, hard look at where we stand.

---

1 Kruse, Kevin. "100 Best Quotes On Leadership." *Forbes*, Forbes Magazine, 18 July 2018, www.forbes.com/sites/kevinkruse/2012/10/16/quotes-on-leadership/#18022b372feb.

A LOOK THROUGH THE LENS

We can put people of influence into three distinct categories: individual stars, limited leaders, and exponential leaders. Which are you?

♦ *Individual stars* are people with great skills, but they don't develop others. Someone might be a concert violinist, a fantastic power forward, a gifted accountant, a brilliant tech specialist, talented department head, or a terrific preacher. Those people have talents I can only dream of (and if it included a plumber or someone with other home repair skills, my wife, Jenni, would be dreaming of me having these talents), but if they don't use their platform to help others learn, grow, and succeed; they're players, not leaders.

♦ *Limited leaders* have an influence in their own sphere of contacts but no further. Most business owners can handle about a hundred employees by themselves, and most churches never grow beyond about 125 people because that's the limit of the leader's ability to personally connect with every person and each family. There's certainly nothing wrong with having a positive impact on 100 people. That's wonderful, but it's a ceiling on a leader's impact unless he learns to develop others as leaders.

♦ *Exponential leaders* have a vision for multiplication. Each employee in the company or family in the church isn't an end; it's a beginning. These leaders invest their time and energy in people who show potential, not only to work or serve well, but to catch the vision to keep multiplying multipliers.

As I explained these categories to a friend, he asked, "But Scott, aren't some people just wired to lead a smaller number of people? Everyone isn't a Jeff Bezos!"

He might have thought I was hedging when I answered, "Well, yes and no. Obviously, some people are more gifted than others, better communicators, more organized, or have more passion for a purpose, but the categories aren't about the level of talent—they're about the scope of a person's vision. I believe every person can become an exponential leader. Every. Single. One."

Our success isn't defined by our frenetic busyness, but by the number of people we've enlisted, equipped, placed, and empowered to have a powerful impact on others.

We need a clearer picture of our role as leaders. It's not to fill the seats or sell products; it's to help the people we touch reach their full potential—and their full potential always has an exponential impact. The problem is that many of us have never seen a picture like this, so we don't know it's possible. And even if we believe it's possible, we don't know how to make it happen.

We need a different measuring stick. Our success isn't defined by people looking to us for answers, but by how wide our sphere of influence has grown so that people look to many more leaders for answers. Our success isn't defined by our frenetic busyness, but by the number of people we've enlisted, equipped, placed, and empowered to have a powerful impact on others.

Our success isn't defined by people seeing us as Superman or Wonder Woman—but when far more people have respect for those who are several layers beyond us on the organizational chart. If it's all about our success, we're losing the game, and we've missed the point of God's calling to all believers, no matter what career they follow, to establish His kingdom of love, kindness, and truth "on earth as it is in heaven." Exponential leaders always have their eyes on a much bigger goal than personal advancement or acclaim.

Please don't misunderstand. I'm not demeaning limited leaders in the least. I have the greatest respect for them. They're often the most compassionate, dedicated people in a community. They serve tirelessly, and they have a profound impact on people. I'm not asking them to add more items to their to-do lists. Actually, if they can develop the mentality and the skills of exponential leadership, they can become less harried and hurried because others will share the load with them.

LEARNING CURVE

My first job was working with young people in a church while I was in college, and I saw myself as an individual star. I was insecure and terrified that I'd fail, and I compensated by trying to control people so they'd contribute to the success of my ministry. Notice: *my* ministry.

I saw them as cogs in my machine. I delegated, but not primarily to develop them. My vision for ministry wasn't to empower people to be effective leaders and expand the scope of our influence. I just wanted them to make me look good.

One day I had the distinct impression I should write down how I thought people perceived me. I had heard a pastor ask the question: "If you were to die today, what would people say about you?" I used that question as my jumping off point. I picked up my pen and wrote, "dynamic," "leader," "strong," "gifted," "passionate," and a few other words. After about the eighth one, I looked at the list and thought, "Cool! That's exactly the reputation I want."

At that moment, a question came to mind that I'm pretty sure was from God Himself: "Where's love on your list?"

I looked again at the list, and I thought, *I just wrote what I want people to say about me, and what I think a lot of people would say, but love didn't make the list. There's something wrong—very wrong—about that.*

Instantly, I realized I was trying to project an image of success instead of truly caring for the people God had entrusted to me. I picked up my pen again. I marked through all the words on my list, and I wrote "LOVE" over all the scribbles. At that moment I made a commitment that loving people well would be my vision, my goal, and my hope for the rest of my life. To make it very practical, I've made it my goal that in every encounter, I want people to walk away from me feeling loved, believed in, encouraged, and built-up. This, I realized later, is how God has always wanted me to influence people. And much later, I understood love is both the fuel and the goal of exponential leadership. I can't be the kind of leader God wants me to be unless I have *their* best interests at heart, not *mine*. From that time until today, when I preach, I'm not speaking so people will appreciate what a wonderful orator I am; I'm speaking so each person grasps the grace of God so deeply that they live to communicate His love to everyone they know. Of course, I want my sermons to be well crafted and powerful, but the goal of my study isn't to bring attention to me. This perspective changed me, my motives, my vision for each message, my words, and ultimately, my impact.

Multiplication has always been God's strategy to impart His grace to every corner of the globe—it's not just a New Testament concept! "Generations" applies to literal generations of families, and it relates to expanding layers of impact. The Scriptures identify God as "the God of Abraham, Isaac, and Jacob" (Genesis 28:14-15), but the generational influence didn't end there. When the psalmist Asaph recounts the history of God's people, he explains how truth and grace are to be passed down:

> [God] decreed statutes for Jacob
>   and established the law in Israel,
> which he commanded our ancestors
>   to teach their children,
> so the next generation would know them,

even the children yet to be born,
    and they in turn would tell their children.
Then they would put their trust in God
    and would not forget his deeds
    but would keep his commands. —Psalm 78:5-7

Multiplication has always been God's strategy to impart His grace to every corner of the globe— it's not just a New Testament concept!

When we first see the Apostle Paul in Luke's history of the early church, he was a destroyer. His passion for God was misguided, and he led the zealous Jewish persecution of believers. Later, though, we see a very different leader. The individual star had become an exponential leader. Everywhere he went, he launched new churches. He appointed elders who led people to lead people. He spelled it out in his second letter to his protégé, Timothy: "And the things you have heard me say in the presence of many witnesses entrust to reliable people who will also be qualified to teach others" (2 Timothy 2:2). He was telling Timothy to do more than gather individuals around him, so they could soak up God's truth. He wanted Timothy to empower "reliable" and "qualified" people who would multiply their impact on countless others. We see four generations in this verse! The phenomenal story of the early church shows that Timothy wasn't the only young leader who adopted Paul's expansive vision of multiplication.

BOTTLENECK

Leading people is as much about our hearts as our heads and our hands. As leaders, we replicate our vision, behavior, and passion in the lives of those around us, but far too often, we can be driven by pride or fear instead of love. When this happens, we manipulate people instead of motivating them. Do people around us notice the difference? Do we?

Manipulation focuses (primarily or exclusively) on *our* goals and *our* reputations. It is fueled by either fear of not measuring up, so we're driven to prove ourselves or arrogance that we know more than anybody else. We manipulate when we use either a carrot (reward) or a stick (guilt) to control people. This behavior is often excused as "bold leadership," but it ultimately results in resentment, not love and loyalty.

Motivation isn't a hair away from manipulation; it's the polar opposite. When we motivate, we focus on what's best for the person, and we empower people. The fuel is love, not fear. We may reward people, but it's more like a father rewards his child than an employer rewarding an employee. When we motivate people, we tap into what's best about them and what's powerful in them. We set them up for success, and we celebrate more about their success than our own because their success *is* our own. Leadership expert Eric Geiger observes:

> Great leaders—leaders who lead with clarity of mission and values, who rally people around a shared purpose, and who

work to help people find joy in the work—are well-prepared to motivate the new type of employee (assuming there really is a new type of employee, because the best ones have always been intrinsically motivated anyway). Great leaders motivate with the strength of their character and commitment, by uniting people around shared values, and by pointing people to the mission that drives all the activity.[2]

Like produces like. Some of us manipulate because that's the only environment we've experienced and the only example we've seen, and we push this behavior throughout our organizations. Is there any hope for change? Yes, of course. We can learn to treasure people instead of using them, and then they can thrive as exponential leaders as we pour our hearts into them and model outstanding leadership skills.

LESSONS FROM A FATHER-IN-LAW

Moses was a phenomenal man. God had to break him before He could use him, and I'm pretty sure that's the pattern for all of us. You would think it was enough of a challenge for Moses to trust God to perform a series of ten miracles so Pharaoh would let the slaves go free and then to face the prospect of annihilation on the banks of the Red Sea as Pharaoh's army prepared to attack, but as we'd say in Texas, "He ain't seen nuthin' yet!"

God promised His people a land flowing with milk and honey, but it didn't happen quickly enough for the people. Only three days after

2 Geiger, Eric. "Seven Differences Between Motivating and Manipulating." *Eric Geiger*, 5 June 2018, ericgeiger.com/2016/05/seven-differences-between-motivating-and-manipulating/.

they left the banks of the Red Sea, they were walking in the desert, and they couldn't find any water. Talk about a leadership challenge! Moses had to lead two million people through a desert with no water, food, or shelter. Not far into the journey, they were so dissatisfied with Moses' leadership that they wanted to go back to Egypt to resume their previous employment! They complained, "If only we had died by the LORD's hand in Egypt! There we sat around pots of meat and ate all the food we wanted, but you have brought us out into this desert to starve this entire assembly to death" (Exodus 16:3).

God provided manna from heaven, water from a rock, and quail from the skies, but the people still griped about everything. There was one person who tried to do it all, one person who made all the decisions, and one person who represented God to the people … and that person, Moses, was at the end of his rope.

Moses' father-in-law came for a visit, and he noticed the strain on Moses' face. First, he praised God for using Moses to deliver His people, but then he offered some advice. The historian tells us:

> The next day Moses took his seat to serve as judge for the people, and they stood around him from morning till evening. When his father-in-law saw all that Moses was doing for the people, he said, "What is this you are doing for the people? Why do you alone sit as judge, while all these people stand around you from morning till evening?"

Moses answered him, "Because the people come to me to seek God's will. Whenever they have a dispute, it is brought to me, and I decide between the parties and inform them of God's decrees and instructions."

Moses' father-in-law replied, "What you are doing is not good. You and these people who come to you will only wear yourselves out. The work is too heavy for you; you cannot handle it alone. Listen now to me and I will give you some advice, and may God be with you. You must be the people's representative before God and bring their disputes to him. Teach them his decrees and instructions, and show them the way they are to live and how they are to behave. But select capable men from all the people—men who fear God, trustworthy men who hate dishonest gain—and appoint them as officials over thousands, hundreds, fifties and tens. Have them serve as judges for the people at all times, but have them bring every difficult case to you; the simple cases they can decide themselves. That will make your load lighter, because they will share it with you. If you do this and God so commands, you will be able to stand the strain, and all these people will go home satisfied." —Exodus 18:13-23

Jethro didn't walk in and take control. He offered advice, and he told Moses to take his ideas to God and let Him confirm them. I believe we can find four powerful principles in this account:

1) Recognize that the most gifted leaders, even those who are so obviously called, appointed, and empowered by God, cannot and should not try to fulfill their calling on their own. Top leaders of any organization or department are to provide clear direction and vision. Like Jethro told Moses, "You must hear from God on behalf of the people," but the organization suffers when other leaders aren't identified, developed, and empowered. It's not enough to be an individual star or a limited leader.

2) Identify the key influencers and determine the scope of their leadership. Some have an impact on thousands of people, some on hundreds, some on dozens, and some on a few. It's your job and mine to notice them, resource them, and place them where they can have the greatest influence. This is your primary role as a leader.

3) Teach the influencers everything they need to know, equip them with the skills they need, and position them for success. Invest your heart in them so they learn to walk with God and enjoy the life God has for them instead of just filling a slot on the organizational chart. Challenge and inspire them to learn more, sharpen their skills, and work well with others on the team. Create a culture that promotes unity and creativity. Celebrate those who surpass you in their areas of expertise.

4) You don't need to have an impact on every person in your organization, but you need to invest your time in those who can have the greatest impact on others.

The pressures and perplexities of leadership weigh on us. No matter how much we work or how well we lead, some will complain we aren't doing enough. In the wilderness, God's people became experts at griping! In the book of Numbers, "Moses heard the people of every family wailing at the entrance of their tents" (Numbers 11:10). If they'd had social media, you can imagine the posts! Moses had just about had enough. He complained to God, "Why have you brought this trouble on your servant? What have I done to displease you that you put the burden of all these people on me? Did I conceive all these people? Did I give them birth? … I cannot carry all these people by myself; the burden is too heavy for me. If this is how you are going to treat me, please go ahead and kill me—if I have found favor in your eyes—do not let me face my own ruin" (Numbers 11:10-12, 14-15). Moses wanted God to take him out and end his misery! Have you ever been there? Sure you have. So have I.

God's answer wasn't to take Moses' leadership card away from him; it was to expand the pool of gifted leaders. God told him, "Bring me seventy of Israel's elders who are known to you as leaders and officials among the people. Have them come to the tent of meeting, that they may stand there with you. I will come down and speak with you there, and I will take some of the power of the Spirit that is on you and put it on them. They will share the burden of the people with you so that you will not have to carry it alone" (Numbers 11:16-17).

God wasn't calling the elders to start new movements. He was calling them to support Moses in the calling He had given him. They would be an extension of Moses to the rest of the people, and they would support his leadership, much like Aaron and Hur supported his arms during battle so God's people would prevail.

THEY JUST DON'T KNOW

I mentioned I've gotten into CrossFit. The guys I work out with are really advanced. In fact, my friend Dave Christianson even made it to the regional competition—which is a pretty big deal! Compared to Dave and the others I work out with, I'm a novice. (And if there's anything lower than a novice, that's me.) One day, I showed up and looked at the WOD, and as always, my heart sank. I wondered if they'd leave me in the dust again. Actually, I didn't wonder. I already knew they would. But as we went through each exercise, something strange was happening: I was keeping up with them! When it was over, I felt great. I was tired, but I was sure I'd experienced a dramatic physical breakthrough. The guys all said things like, "Great job today, Scott," "Killed it today, man," and "You were on today!"

I said, "That was a hard one today, but I think I did pretty well."

A couple of them replied, "Oh, man, you were great!"

I was about to walk out of the dressing room, but before I left, they took their shirts off. They were wearing 40-pound vests! I was the only one not wearing one.

Like my first, inaccurate view of my CrossFit buddies, most of the people in our organizations don't understand the weight their leader carries. They see us serving, loving, and leading, and they assume it's easy. It's not. Caring is a heavy burden ... on our bodies, our families, and our hearts. In one way, that's fine. We don't want to whine and complain all the time, but you know and I know that we carry weights others just don't see.

For many of us, the burden is magnified by the feeling that we're stuck under the limits of our existing team. We can't imagine building a team of eager, talented, humble, and effective leaders whose influence radiates throughout the organization and into the community.

You're not stuck as a leader. You simply have a choice to make. Do you want to become an exponential leader? I do. I want to help you discover how to increase your leadership influence. That's why I wrote this book.

Leadership, I believe, rests on two factors: respect and relationship. In these pages, we'll look at five ways to increase the level of respect people have for you, and we'll look at five ways to build stronger relationships with them. If you apply these ten lessons, you'll become an exponential leader. These principles enable us to motivate people and avoid the destructive impact of manipulation. In these chapters, you'll find very practical steps to becoming an exponential leader. Of course, these aren't the only ten lessons. They're just the ten I've used and recommend, but as you read, listen, interact, and grow, you'll undoubtedly find many more ideas and uncover better applications. My suggestions are just a starting point for you. In fact, please send me your ideas. I'm always learning, and I'd love to hear from you. You can help me grow, so I can help other leaders grow. This is what I live for.

> *Leadership, I believe, rests on two factors: respect and relationship.*

The principles in these chapters are focused on how you can increase your personal influence with "key influencers" in your organization.

At the end of each chapter, you'll find some reflection questions and exercises to help you apply the principles. Don't rush through these. Sit with them, think about them, talk with others about them, and start working to implement them in your relationships with the people you lead.

THINK ABOUT IT:

1) In your organization, who are the individual stars, the limited leaders, and the exponential leaders?

2) Who are some exponential leaders you look up to?

3) What do you need to do to learn more from them and follow their example?

4) On a scale of 0 (not in the least) to 10 (off the charts), how stuck do you feel with the people on your leadership team? Explain your answer.

Chapter 2

R & R

Not long ago, I talked with a friend who is a pastor about the concepts in this book, and he asked me, "Of the pastors you know, how many are frustrated?"

I responded, "About 90 percent of them." He nodded like he wanted me to explain, so I dove in, "I think that's about the percentage of pastors who are limited leaders, those whose influence stops at the people who are personally connected with them. Their solution, quite often, is to double down and work even harder. This strategy seems noble, but it soon leads to even more frustration … and worse, to burnout." When I talk to pastors, I hear all kinds of complaints, such as:

"If I could just get that guy on my board, things would go much more smoothly."

Or more often, "If I could just get that guy off my board, I could sleep better at night."

"Why is it that every other pastor can find great worship leaders, but I'm stuck with this guy?"

"If the money would come in, we'd be fine."

"The conflict among my key volunteers is killing our momentum. I've tried to resolve it, but nothing works."

"My church can't grow because we're located in a dead part of town."

"You don't understand what I'm up against. My church is in Boston, and the East Coast is a really hard place to build a ministry."

"Our town is so small that 150 people in attendance makes us a megachurch."

In all of these complaints, there's a common thread: Each pastor is convinced the problem is outside of his control, and there's nothing he can do about it. Certainly, there are things outside our control, but almost certainly not as many as we might think. One very important thing is in our hands: the ability to build a network of competent, multiplying leaders. I'm not suggesting we need to ditch the people on our teams and boards. In many cases, they aren't the problem—we are. If we change our perspective and transform our leadership strategy, the people near us right now can become exponential leaders who have an impact on generation after generation of others. We picked (or somebody picked) the people in leadership around us because they already have some influence. Let's capitalize on the heart and talents they already have and infuse them with the vision to become multiplying leaders.

Influence, as I've said, is formed by two factors: respect and relationship. Respect is earned by character and competency. It's the Mechanic's Principle. When people ask if you know a good mechanic, they're asking, "Do you know someone who has the competency to fix my car and I can trust to not overcharge me?" People are asking the same thing about me as a leader. Intuitively, they wonder, *Does he know what he's doing (competency), and can I trust him to lead in a way that is good for me and not just for him (character)?*

Relationships are built as trust is earned. Both take time. When I spend time with people, they know I care about them as individuals who have their own hopes and dreams, not just as wheels that make our organization run. But time alone isn't the answer. If I spend time with people, but they trust me less and despise me more, I've gone backward in my ability to have influence in their lives. Some leaders don't want to hang out with their people because they're afraid of being exposed. They avoid relaxed, friendly times because they don't know how to be a friend. To them, it's all business all the time.

Respect and relationship are the two wings of a leadership airplane. Without both of them, we crash and burn. When we command respect without a relationship of concern, we act like generals ordering our troops into battle—and they'd better obey! We expect (demand) people do what we say. When they do, we give them a bit of praise, and when they don't, we let them know they're on a short leash. These are leaders who may be brilliant in strategy or platform skills, but they have a polarizing effect on others—followers are either fiercely loyal to "the strong man" or resentful of the overbearing boss. When talented people find another place where a boss values *them* as well as their expertise, they're gone in a heartbeat.

On the other hand, relationship without respect makes us good friends but not great leaders. People may enjoy hanging out with us, but they won't follow us. When we're disorganized, when we settle for mediocrity, and when we don't have a clear plan, people drift away— or run as fast as they can.

Years ago, my father gave me a glimpse into our family's past. He told me that his father, who was a pastor, never stayed at a church for more than three years. When I asked, "What was that about?" he explained, "Whenever anyone on his board disagreed with him, that person immediately went on a blacklist in his mind and heart. My dad wouldn't let that person ever have any influence ever again. But after he marked off the four or five people who had real influence in his church, they marked him off, and he had to find another church."

My grandfather was tremendously threatened by anyone else who had influence, and his insecurity wrecked his ability to lead. My father was determined to avoid my grandfather's mistakes, but the model was so powerful that Dad always struggled to trust people on his staff team and board. If anything, I've gone to the other end of the continuum. I'm an open book, and I'm genuinely thrilled when leaders in our church express their feelings and opinions (well, most of the time.)

Respect and relationship are the two wings of a leadership airplane. Without both of them, we crash and burn.

This positive assumption about leaders in our church gives me a wide open door to connect with them in meaningful ways. Our family has shown some progress over the generations. My grandfather was defensive toward anyone who raised an eyebrow, much less disagreed with him in a meeting. My father knew it was important to make real connections with leaders, but he always struggled with suspicions that they weren't really loyal. I've found that respect and relationship aren't optional equipment; they're absolutely necessary for our organization to run on all cylinders. And my sons and people on our team? They're taking all this to the next level.

Let's look at two key steps before we dive into the ten practical strategies: identify the influencers and evaluate the influence you have with them.

STEP 1: IDENTIFY THE INFLUENCERS

They're already there. Most are probably in positions of leadership, but some have untitled but very real power. Jack Mourning is a member of our church. He's an architect by training, and he became so successful, he retired with the title, Senior Vice President of Global Development for Fidelity Investments. He was the senior project manager over all the sub project managers throughout the world for the investment firm, and he knows construction inside and out. Whether he's on our board or not is irrelevant. His expertise and the respect he has earned from leaders in our church give him a powerful voice. I always go to him for input on any building project, from the first idea to the buildout. When he gives his opinion, I listen, our board listens, and big givers in the congregation listen.

I talked to a pastor about identifying the influencers in his church, and he immediately responded, "I haven't done a very good job relating to our top givers."

I told him, "Wait a minute. I'm not sure why you immediately jumped to money. You have a lot of people who are influential but don't give a lot of money. You need to notice who they are and how they already contribute."

What does an influencer look like in your organization?
Here are some diagnostic questions:

1) Who are the ones people listen to because they've earned respect and people like them?

2) Who are the ones people go to when they have a hard question?

3) Who are the ones people contact when they want to know the inside scoop?

4) Whose shoulders do people cry on when they're upset?

5) Who are the ones who organize people to accomplish tasks?

6) Who are the ones who bring the most resources—money, people, or expertise—to meet the needs of the organization?

How can you come up with a good list of influencers?
I wanted to get the input of everyone on our staff team, so I devised this strategy:

1) In a staff meeting, I explained what I was doing and why it's important to identify existing influencers, and I asked each of them to come the next week with their list of the top ten in our church. No staff members could be on our lists.

2) The next week, I asked the first person to give me the names on her list. I wrote these on a white board.

3) I asked the next person to give me the names of anyone who wasn't already on the list I was making.

4) I went around the room adding the names of those on the individual lists who hadn't made it to the composite list. At that point, we had about 40 names.

5) I asked each person on our team to list their top five from the 40 and rank them one through five. (I went over the six diagnostic questions to help them evaluate the impact of each one.)

6) I went around the room asking each person for their list of five, and I put a tic mark next to each name that was called. I added the marks, which showed us who we consider the most influential people in our church. We did this one more time, and that gave us a list of the top ten influencers in the church.

7) I told our people to take a picture of the list on the board, and I announced, "You've identified these as having the biggest impact on the people in our church. Know their names, return their calls and emails—immediately, and always respond with professionalism and kindness. If any of them are in your department, take special note of that fact."

8) There were two important groups that were unrepresented or underrepresented: young leaders and African Americans. Young people are the future of any church, but they're often overlooked—or seen in a negative light—by older generations who have been serving in the church for a long time. I believe it's crucial for every church to have an effective strategy to attract and involve young people, and out of this pool, look for rising leaders. Our church already had a significant number of Latinos in leadership positions, so we didn't need to make any special effort there, but the demographics around our church showed an increasing population of African Americans. Forty-five percent of those who are new to our church are African American, and we needed to make some adjustments to be sure

we could minister effectively to them. If we're not intentional about raising up leaders who look like them, we'll miss a terrific opportunity.

9) I asked every person on our staff team to use the same process with the teams in their departments so they can focus attention on existing influencers, young leaders, and African Americans. So, they have two lists: one for the whole church and one for their area of ministry.

As I looked at the list, I felt our team had done a really good job of identifying the people who make the most difference in our church, but I also asked myself a few questions:

1) Was there anyone on the short list that surprised me? If someone did, it means that my staff team thinks more highly of that person than I normally do. If that's the case, I need to pay attention because my staff may see something that I've missed.

2) Was anyone left off the short list that surprised me? This time, it was a sign that I thought more highly of someone than my staff did.

3) Should anyone be added because they have influence that our staff may not appreciate? The answer is "Yes!" Some of the people who give the most to our church aren't very visible, and I added them. I gave these names to our team and told them, "You don't see what this person does for our church, but I do. Whether you've noticed the impact this person has or not, he's on my top ten, and if he's on my list, I want him on your list, too. And by the way, this man's contribution pays the salaries and

expenses of five of you. Now are you putting him on your list? Yeah, I thought so. "

4) If we're intentional about raising up leaders from the younger generation and an under-represented ethnic group, what shifts in the existing organizational chart need to be made? Who needs to focus on one of these groups? What resources need to be allocated for this emphasis?

5) Are any people who have positions in the church not on the list? If that's the case, it tells me a lot about how our staff team views them.

If your organization doesn't have a staff team, work through this process with your board. And if you don't have anybody you can ask, do this exercise yourself. If you're leading a small business, nonprofit, or church, you undoubtedly know who you can count on. The rule of thumb is to identify at least ten people as influencers, or maybe your top 10 percent.

It's very important our entire staff team recognizes the top influencers in our church. Let me put it this way: It frustrates me to death when one of my top influencers tells me he's called one of our staff several times and hasn't gotten a response, or he's asked a question and hasn't gotten a thorough answer. That's unacceptable, and it will happen far less if the people on our team understand the impact these influencers have.

Write the names of your top ten influencers. (You may want to write more than ten and then determine the ten.)

STEP 2: EVALUATE THE LEVEL OF INFLUENCE

This is a fun (and perhaps revealing) exercise. Write down your list of top ten influencers, and assign a score from 0 (a total dud) to 10 (off the charts) for the respect you've earned and the relationship you've built, and then add the two together for the influence score. For instance:

Ken

    Respect 6
    Relationship 7
    Influence score 13

Jack

    Respect 5
    Relationship 4
    Influence score 9

Scoring for Respect

10 You're the greatest leader of all time

7 He admires you

5 He sees you as a peer

3 He has questions about your competency

0 He wants to buy you a bus ticket

Scoring for Relationship

10 You're his dearest friend

7 He loves you

5 He tolerates you

3 He really doesn't click with you

0 His stomach churns at the thought of you

Top Ten Influencers

Name: _____

Respect_____   Relationship_____   Influence score_____

Name: _____

Respect_____   Relationship_____   Influence score_____

Name: _____

Respect_____   Relationship_____   Influence score_____

Name: _____

Respect_____   Relationship_____   Influence score_____

Name: _____

Respect_____   Relationship_____   Influence score_____

Name: _____

Respect_____ Relationship_____ Influence score_____

Name: _____

Respect_____ Relationship_____ Influence score_____

Name: _____

Respect_____ Relationship_____ Influence score_____

Name: _____

Respect_____ Relationship_____ Influence score_____

Name: _____

Respect_____ Relationship_____ Influence score_____

Your total influence score (add the total of all ten): _____

Read the scoring summary (below) that corresponds with this score.

STEP 3: SCORING SUMMARIES

Add the ten influence scores. A perfect score would be 200. (If that's your score, you need some work on objectivity!) After totaling your score find where you are currently in your leadership, and take a minute to read my personal message to you.

0 to 50 A New or Struggling Leader

Don't be discouraged. I'm going to help you grow in your influence with your top ten, but I can't do it for you. Soak up the principles in this book and apply them. Your leadership and the future of your church depend on it.

51 to 100 Potential Leader

Look at the ones where your score is low. I'm going to show you how to improve both of the scores for respect and relationship, and you'll make great progress. You can do this!

101 to 125 Good Leader

You've got a huge opportunity here! I'm so glad you picked up this book. I'm going to show you how to raise the score for each of your top ten at least one point (and maybe two) in the next six months.

126 to 150 Gifted Leader

Make your top ten influencers a high priority in your schedule and your heart for the next six to 12 months. It will make a huge difference for you and your church. You already have a lot of credibility with them. Build on it.

151 to 175 Dynamic Leader

Wow! Well done! You have a ton of influence with your influencers. Now you can focus on teaching them to grow their influence with others to expand their impact (and yours) to more generations.

176 to 200 Leader of Leaders

Please write a book on leadership. I'll buy a box full!

1) As you look at your scoring summary, what stands out to you?

2) What's the obvious pattern?

3) Are there any concerns? Holes? Bombs?

My assurances in the summaries about helping you raise your influence quotient aren't empty. I've seen leaders make major gains as they've learned some foundational principles of multiplying the multipliers.

Some of you may be discouraged at this point. I want to assure you that you can make real progress. You aren't stuck with the status quo. You can earn far more respect, and you can build far richer, deeper relationships.

(I asked the people on our staff team to use the same process with their top ten.)

WHERE WE'RE GOING

Now that you have identified your top ten leaders, and you've assessed the current level of influence you have with each of them, I want to help you have even greater influence. This is my promise: If you'll apply the principles in the rest of the book to your top ten, you'll get amazing results. Let me give you an overview of where we're going:

Five ways to earn respect

1) Meet and exceed expectations.
2) Lead with honest and consistent communication.
3) Develop a process for wise decision making.
4) Model the importance of personal growth.
5) Fix your own problems.

Five ways to build relationships

1) Speak their "language."
2) Remember what they've said.
3) Value whom they value.
4) Capitalize on the most important moments in their lives.
5) Add value with no strings attached.

Our next stop: Earning the respect of your key influencers.

THINK ABOUT IT:

1) How do you feel at the end of this chapter? Discouraged? Hopeful? Committed?

2) How do you think your team or key volunteers will respond to the exercises in this chapter?

3) When will you use these exercises?

4) As you named your top ten influencers and evaluated your connection with them, what did the exercise tell you about your influence on these people? (What's the good, the bad, and the confusing?)

5) What are some areas of strength?

6) What needs to improve?

Part 2

Five Ways to Earn Respect

Chapter 3

MEET AND EXCEED EXPECTATIONS

In the last chapter, you identified your top ten influencers. Before you get any farther in this chapter, write down the names of any of these people who are less than happy with you right now. You can write their initials or their first names, or give them nicknames, or maybe write in code. You never know who's thumbing through your book!

Got it? Good. Now you're ready for this chapter.

What is the main reason people get frustrated with you? Come on, it's not that hard to figure out. I'm not talking about a particular quirk in your personality or a single instance when you dropped the ball. If you step back and look at the grimaces, shaking heads, and mumbled (or shouted) complaints, they all have one thing in common: You failed to meet someone's specific expectations.

You can count on the fact that people have them. They have a measuring stick for every staff meeting, every board meeting, every budget, every activity, the way you look, the way you act, and the way you smell. (Well, let's hope that's not something they need to notice!) When you miss the mark, you lose their respect.

Whenever anyone is frustrated with me, I've learned to ask, "What expectation have I failed to meet?" It happens in every area of my life.

If I tell Jenni I'll be home for dinner at 6:00, but I come through the door at 7:00, how would you expect her to feel? I don't have to guess. She'd be frustrated … and leaning toward ticked! The first thing I'd notice is there's nothing on the table because the leftovers would already be in the refrigerator in several of those handy snap-lid plastic containers. I'd try to be cheerful and act like nothing was wrong, but I assure you, it wouldn't work. I'd say, "Hey, honey," but before I could say another word, she'd ask, "Where have you been? Do you know what time it is? I thought you said you'd be home at 6:00. And by the way, dinner was delicious."

My high-performance brain is adept at making excuses, so I'd dive in: "I know, Babe, but you know how it goes. I was headed to my car at 5:45, but James said he really needed to talk to me. As soon as we were through, I remembered I'd left something in the office. I went back to get it, but Tammy flagged me down and asked me to read over a really important letter I gave her to send. It needed to be just right, and it had to go out today. When I handed it back to her, I realized it was almost 7:00, so I ran—literally *ran*—in the parking lot to my car. I'm glad the State Patrol didn't stop me on the way home because I was flying! I got here just as fast as I could. You understand that, don't you, Sweetheart?"

At that moment, I would try to inch my way closer to her so I could hug her and make everything all better, but she would have nothing of it! She'd say, "Don't you try to hug your way out of this. You could at least have called to tell me you were going to be late!"

I'd try to worm my way out of trouble again: "You're right. It was so thoughtless of me, but my phone wouldn't stop ringing, and I didn't have a single minute that someone didn't need me."

You can imagine how the rest of the evening would have gone ... and Jenni is undoubtedly the sweetest, nicest, most compassionate person I've ever known!

Now, think through this interaction and notice what happened:

- We had agreed on the expectation that I'd be home at 6:00.

- There was a gap between Jenni's expectation ("I'll be home at 6:00.") and reality (I showed up at 7:00).
- Making excuses only works if the failure to meet expectations is rare and minor.
- The problem could have been easily resolved with a quick phone call right before or after 6:00. And if I'd called any time before I got home, it would at least have shown a tiny bit of responsibility and care.

When we fail to meet others' expectations,
their respect for us leaks.

Whenever reality is less than what people expect, we lose ground. However, if I'd made the phone call to Jenni, I would have managed her expectation, bringing it closer to reality. This is how I see it:

Expectation

↕ The size of the gap is the measure of others' frustration with us.

Disappointing Reality

Jenni was saying, in effect, "If you'd called, the gap between my expectation and reality would at least have been narrower … and that would be a big improvement!"

Sometimes, the problem is we failed to meet an expectation we've defined. We said we'd have a report by the next board meeting, but we didn't have it. We said the Christmas event would be spectacular, but it was mediocre. We told investors the revenue would rebound in the last quarter, but it didn't. Other times, people are frustrated because we didn't give them clear expectations. We weren't very clear about what we were going to do, maybe because we wanted the wiggle room in case there was a delay or something didn't work out like we'd hoped. However, failing to communicate goals creates confusion, which inevitably produces frustration of its own kind.

MANAGING EXPECTATIONS

When we fail to meet others' expectations, their respect for us leaks. Managing expectations doesn't build respect, but it goes a long way to keep it from leaking. The solution, as we've seen, isn't to avoid goals, timelines, and a vision for something better. Respect is built when we set clear and attainable goals, communicate progress, and reach them.

When I was called to be the lead pastor at our church, I certainly wasn't an unknown quantity. I'd been the youth pastor and associate pastor for 14 years, but this was a new role for me, and it changed how our board viewed me. I intuitively knew that I needed to clarify their expectations, so I walked into the meeting with a stack of three-by-five index cards.

I started the meeting in prayer, and then I told them I was very thankful for the opportunity to be their pastor. I voiced my commitment to serve them and the church to the best of my ability. I then said, "I want to be sure I meet, and hopefully exceed, your expectations. I want to know how you'll be keeping score next year when you evaluate my leadership. With that in mind, it would be very helpful—to me, at least, and maybe for you, too—for us to have the same scorecard."

I gave each of them an index card, and I asked them to take a few minutes to write down the responsibilities they considered most important for the lead pastor at Oaks Church. It was obvious they had plenty of ideas about this topic because they immediately began to make their lists. After a few minutes, I collected them and handed them to the church secretary. I told him, "Now, if you don't mind, call them out and write them on a whiteboard. I'm sure there are some duplicates. You don't need to write any of them twice ... just include any that aren't already up there."

We watched as he looked at each card and wrote specific expectations. At 25, a few people chuckled. When he was finished, there were 39 items on the board. By that point, he had to write smaller and then sideways to include them all. By then, everyone was laughing ... everyone but me. I knew the weight of their expectations would crush me because no one could meet all of them.

I went down the list one by one, asking for clarification. I said, "Here's 'visit the sick in the hospital.' That certainly needs to be done, but are you saying that *I'm the one* who needs to visit every person who's sick, or can other people make these visits, too? I know it's important that people feel loved and cared for, but I need to understand if you think I should be the one to visit sick people each week?"

The board members were quick to jump in. Several of them said something like, "Oh, no, it doesn't have to be you, as long as someone does it and does it well."

"Great," I responded, and I erased that one off the list. (By the way, this was a monumental shift. The pastor before my dad saw hospital visits as his primary responsibility. He came to the church for a half hour for devotions in the morning, then spent most of the day at the hospital and nursing homes. He came back to the church in the late afternoon to take care of anything he'd missed that day—and this was his pattern almost every day. The expectations of virtually everyone in the church were that I would follow that example. This change may not seem like a big deal to you, but I assure you, it was a very big deal to me!)

I pointed to another one on the board. "What about 'teach on Wednesday nights'? Do *I need to speak* every time? Can someone who is gifted and effective teach on at least some of these times?"

"Sure, of course," several of them said. So I erased that one.

I held the eraser next to another one: "Okay, this says, 'Be available to counsel individuals and couples.' Is this something *I'm solely responsible* to do, or can this be performed by a skilled counselor or gifted pastor?" I paused for a second and told them, "And besides, I don't think you want me doing too much of this anyway. I'm terrible at counseling!"

They laughed, and one of them spoke for them all: "You're right. We definitely need to find someone else!"

We needed to rethink our direction, our assumptions, and our expectations to focus on multiplying multipliers, not just for me to work myself to death.

I erased it from the board. After going through the entire list, there were only four responsibilities left that only I could do:

1) Vision: Provide direction for the church.
2) Funding: Make sure we stay within the budget.
3) Staff: Manage all our personnel.
4) Preaching: Be the primary communicator on the weekend.

Sometimes I look back on an event and think, *Lord, I had no idea how important this would be, but You saved me from a world of trouble by leading me to do that!* If we hadn't had this conversation, there would have been multiple scorecards—everyone in the room would have had their own. If I'd tried to meet all of them, I would have pleased some and disappointed others. I would have been whipsawed back and forth by their approval and disapproval on virtually every decision I made. Having a single scorecard clarified expectations and gave me the opportunity to gain the respect of the board.

At many churches, the board and other top leaders assume they've hired the pastor to do everything—literally everything. I'm not sure if any of our board members would have actually said I was responsible for doing everything—probably few if any—but it was tremendously important for us to get on the same page about the scope of my responsibilities. In this meeting, God led me to manage their expectations and bring them much closer to reality. My role isn't to do all the work; my task is to "equip the saints for the work of ministry" (Ephesians 4:11-12).

At the time, the biggest obstacle to our church breaking the 1,000 barriers was our lack of a strategy to develop lay leaders. Before this discussion, several of the people on our board had concluded I just needed to work harder and do more. I could have tried, but I don't know where I'd be today if that had been my strategy. We needed to rethink our direction, our assumptions, and our expectations to focus on multiplying multipliers, not just for me to work myself to death. This meeting was, in my estimation, a pivotal moment in the history of our church … and certainly in my life.

This principle is vital, too, on a personal level. I told my counselor sometimes when Jenni tells me about a problem, I jump in with a solution, but she says, "Wait! I don't want you to fix it. I only want you to listen." But sometimes, I have the good sense just to listen, but she tells me, "Are you going to just sit there and let me talk? Say something!"

My counselor related, "It's confusing, isn't it?" I nodded. He continued, "The trick is to manage Jenni's expectation upfront. When she wants to talk to you about something important, ask, 'Do you want me to just listen, or do you want me to help you fix the problem?'"

"Cool. That makes perfect sense," I replied.

He smiled, "Sometimes she doesn't know if she just wants you to listen or if she wants you to weigh in on a solution. But when she commits to one or the other at the beginning of the conversation, it puts you on the same page. This solves a lot of communication problems in marriage."

EXCEEDING EXPECTATIONS

When reality exceeds expectations, we earn tons of respect. Here's what it looks like:

- Delivering *more than* what was expected.

What if we not only stayed in budget but could give raises, increase the amount in savings, and contribute to some local projects in the community? That's more!

- Doing things *better than* expected.

What if we developed the staff so they were more effective? What if we resolved a long-simmering conflict among staff? What if we took the time to vet new hires and found new staff members who are outstanding in their roles? That's better!

♦ Doing things *faster than* expected.

What if a building project that was scheduled to be completed in two years was finished in eighteen months? What if we could roll out a new program sooner than anyone anticipated? That's faster!

When we redraw the diagram about expectations, we include a new line above expectations. The gap at the bottom is all about the level of frustration, but the gap at the top is when people say, "Wow! That's fantastic! It's so much more, so much better, and so much faster than I ever imagined!"

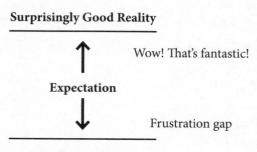

Surprisingly Good Reality

Wow! That's fantastic!

Expectation

Frustration gap

Disappointing Reality

Others' respect for you *erodes* when you fail to meet their expectations, it remains *relatively constant* when you consistently meet the expectations, and it *grows* to the degree that you exceed expectations. It's totally unrealistic (and probably obsessive-compulsive) to think you can exceed expectations all the time. It's just not going to happen.

Here's how I see my goals:

- ◆ All day every day, I do what I say I'll do, I do it with excellence, and I do it on time. That's meeting expectations.

- ◆ As soon as I realize my stated goals aren't going to be met, I manage expectations by communicating to the team and take steps to limit the damage.

- ◆ I look at the goals and activities for the quarter. I pick two or three of the most significant ones, and try like crazy to exceed expectations.

This is a framework I've used for years. At first, I had to write it down and think hard about meeting, managing, and exceeding expectations, but now, it's second nature. It can become that for you, too.

THINK ABOUT IT:

1) Today, where on the diagram would you put each of the people on your list of top ten influencers?

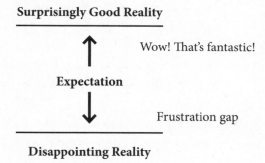

Surprisingly Good Reality

Wow! That's fantastic!

Expectation

Frustration gap

Disappointing Reality

2) Are any of them frustrated with you? If so, what is the specific expectation of each one that you're not meeting?

3) What does it mean to be skilled at managing the expectations of others? Who do you know who does it well? What can you learn from that person?

4) Would it help to hand out index cards and have a conversation with your leaders like I had with my board? Explain your answer.

5) What are some ways you can exceed expectations …

◆ at home with your spouse and children?

◆ in your next meeting (for instance, bring a gift, finish early, take them to lunch, tell them what you appreciate about them)?

◆ in your presentations (for instance, make a video instead of giving handouts, tell stories instead of just stats)?

◆ in your projects (for instance, do more, do better, and get it done faster than anyone expects)?

Chapter 4

KEEP THEM IN THE KNOW

A pastor called me on a Monday morning. He was really upset. He said, "Scott, I don't know what I'm going to do with these people?"

"What people?" I asked.

"It feels like a mutiny!"

I tried again: "And who are the rebels?"

"Just about everybody."

At that point, I decided to take a different route. "Tell me what happened."

He launched in: "Yesterday, I announced in our service that we were moving away from the traditional Sunday school model and starting small groups in people's homes. You would have thought I'd slashed all their tires in the parking lot! After the service, I could hardly get out of the building. They lined up to blast me!"

I asked, "Did your board and Sunday school teachers back you?"

There was silence for a few seconds, and then he almost yelled, "Scott, don't you get it? They were the ones who were most upset!"

"So … you didn't get their buy-in before you made the announcement?"

"Why should I?" His frustration had turned to defensiveness. "I'm the leader. It's my decision."

I wanted to tell him this was a self-inflicted wound, but I decided to be a bit more subtle: "I understand that you're the leader and it's your decision, but you could have gotten your leaders on board and avoided the blowback yesterday if you'd taken the time to discuss the proposal with them before you made the announcement—and people who had questions could have gone to them, not just to you. Does that make sense?"

I could feel his anger at me. In a very low tone of voice, he said, "Scott, that's not the way we do things around here."

Exactly.

TWO BUCKETS

I've had countless conversations with leaders in business and the non-profit world who can't understand why their staff members and board are "so negative," "complain all the time," or "are always finding fault with every decision I make." When I probe a little, I almost always find the leader has announced decisions without taking the time to explain the idea to influencers to get them on board. When key leaders are blindsided, they use their influence to push back instead of supporting the new direction. And the people they influence look to them for cues about how to respond, so complaints ripple through the organization.

When the pastor announced the church would no longer have Sunday school, where did the eyes of people in the congregation go? To the Sunday school teachers in the room! Their facial expressions of exasperation, confusion, and anger communicated loudly and clearly to the people who faithfully sit in their classes.

It's not enough to just inform influencers of your decisions—they need to be included in the process of decision making. Here's the truth: If you don't even tell them before you make an announcement, you can expect major blowback. If you tell them but don't engage them in the deliberations, they may grudgingly accept your decision, but they won't be cheerleaders. But before you make an announcement, if you take the time to meet with them, share your heart, listen to their input, and make adjustments based on their wisdom, they'll almost certainly have your back. If this sounds like "it takes too much time," don't kid yourself. Putting out fires takes much more time, and worse, the drama reduces their respect for you.

Every influencer has two buckets: One is filled with water and the other with gas. When people they influence are on fire and come to them after you've announced a new strategy, the influencer will pour one of the buckets on them. The bucket they choose is directly related to how much you've included them in the process.

Let me illustrate this point with two scenarios. Both have the same public message: I stand up on Sunday morning and announce that our church is starting a new campus in a nearby community.

Scenario #1

I attended a conference where I heard pastors of remarkable multisite churches talk about how many people they were reaching and discipling. I was so excited that I was sure it must be God's plan for us, too. When I made the announcement, I expected a wave of applause, "Amens," and smiles. That was the response of some people, but noticeably, not my board members. They looked at me like I'd lost my mind. I overheard some people talking to one of the key guys on the board after the service. All I could make out was him saying, "Yeah, it's a surprise to me, too. I had no idea this was even a thought, much less a plan. How is he going to pay for it? Who will lead it? I don't know what's going on, but I'll find out."

What do you think those people were thinking and feeling when they walked away from the board member? Not exactly hopeful and excited! He poured gas on the situation and made it worse.

The bucket they choose is directly related to how much you've included them in the process.

Scenario #2

I attended a conference where I heard pastors of remarkable multi-site churches talk about how many people they were reaching and discipling. I was so excited that I was sure it must be God's plan for us, too. (Sound familiar?) I had lunches and coffee with each of the people on our board to share the idea and ask for their input. They asked great questions about leadership at the new campus, the budget, and how it would affect our church if 100 or so of our people attended there for a while to help it launch. In the next board meeting, we talked about it again, and we outlined a timeline and benchmarks, first for the decision, a "go or no go," and if we went forward, how we would answer the obvious questions of why, how, when, where, and who. After several months and lots of discussions and prayer, our board was all in. Two weeks later, I made the announcement in church, and I asked three board members to share their vision for the new campus. When they finished, I concluded, "We've been planning behind the scenes for several months. We have the money, we have the leadership, and we have a launch team of about a hundred people from our church to help lead the new venture. We're confident this is what God is leading us to do. Let's pray together that God will do wonders there."

After the service, the board members are mobbed by people in the congregation. Most of them were coming to ask how they could help make the vision successful. There were still some who weren't happy, but when they approached the board members with questions and concerns, the leaders were able to answer every question with great confidence, and in doing so, they poured water on the fire and put it out.

Business leaders and pastors must respect the power of "cascading communication" in launching a new product or strategy. It works like this:

- The leader takes the time to get the buy-in of top influencers.
- Then the leader takes a few of the top influencers to communicate the concept to the next level of leaders. This level realizes the top influencers are on board, which gives them confidence that "it has legs."
- Then the leader takes one or two of the top influencers and a couple of people from the next level of leaders to share the idea with the third level of leaders. By now, lots of questions have been asked, and almost every problem has been thoroughly resolved.
- Then and only then does the leader make the broad announcement to everyone.

At each level, people are invited to ask questions and enter a dialogue. When their questions and concerns are valued, people feel validated, and they're more eager to support the new idea and participate by serving and giving.

In an article for the Center for Management & Organization Effectiveness, the author explains the cascading principle, which works just as well in churches as it does in the business world:

> Whenever your leadership team reaches a decision that will have a significant impact on the workforce, the next step is to decide on how to cascade the message. Before the meeting is adjourned, make sure that all leaders are clear on the details of the announcement and their responsibility for communicating it to the workforce.
>
> When a message is relayed to mid-level and frontline leaders, it's important to give them the opportunity to ask questions, share their concerns, and make suggestions. During this step in the communication process, they should be allowed to share their opinions and ideas. This is the only way to gain the full support and commitment of mid-level leaders, especially because they may initially disagree with the decision that has been made.
>
> Having a two-way conversation ensures that each person will be able to move forward and commit to supporting the

implementation process, regardless of whether they agree with the decision.[3]

One of my biggest frustrations is I sometimes fail to follow leadership principles I teach and write about. Recently, I made an announcement to our board, but I hadn't run the idea by any of them before we met as a group. I'd been running fast (What's new about that?), and I'd been traveling (ditto.), and I thought I'd talked to at least some of them, but it just hadn't happened. When I made the bold pronouncement, I got the reaction I've described earlier: arms crossed, frowns, and looks of frustration. It didn't take long for the light bulb to come on. I asked, "You, uh, you didn't know anything about this, did you?"

What would create a culture of support where people believe they can say virtually anything and still be valued?

They shook their heads, then one of them said, "We'll give you a pass. This hardly ever happens. We're good."

I was very, very grateful for the grace shown to me. I'm convinced they wouldn't have been so understanding if this had been a regular occurrence.

---

3 "Cascading Communication: Sending Out Your Message to the Entire Organization." *CMOE*, 18 Nov. 2019, cmoe.com/blog/cascading-communication-sending-message-entire-organization/.

HONESTY: GIVING AND RECEIVING

When I became the lead pastor at our church, we suffered from a strong undercurrent of fault-finding, which was expressed in seemingly rampant gossip. (I hope you can't relate, but my guess is that most of you can.) I tried to figure out what was going on. Certainly, sharing secrets is exciting, and forming alliances makes people feel powerful. Whatever the cause, I knew it had to stop. But how?

I asked myself, *What would create a culture of support where people believe they can say virtually anything and still be valued? What would promote and sustain trust among the people on the team?* As I thought about it, three fears appeared to be present in the people on our team:

- ◆ The fear that an honest comment would be laughed at, ridiculed, or ignored;
- ◆ The fear that the person speaking would be perceived as a trouble-maker; and
- ◆ The fear that nothing they said would make a difference because no one would listen anyway.

To calm these fears and give people confidence that their opinions would be valued, we implemented an "honesty policy." As always, it began with me. I wrote out a covenant statement that all of the leaders could agree to and sign:

> "I will speak the truth in love to the last 10 percent, to the right person, at the right time, and in the right way. And I will not engage in or tolerate gossip of any kind."

This policy would be meaningless if I weren't committed to lead it and model it. It would have been just another pious platitude that actually erodes respect instead of building it. When I told our staff team and our board about this policy, I invited them to be completely honest with me about things they see that I don't see, things they've tried to tell me that I don't seem to hear, and times when I don't understand people, ideas, construction, building codes, and financial strategies. These are blind spots, deaf spots, and dumb spots in my life. I told them, "You might hurt my feelings by speaking the truth to me, but you'll hurt me worse if you don't. I'm inviting you to speak into my life, so I can become a better person and a better leader. I would rather you tell me the truth, the hard truth, and give me the opportunity to change than to let me stay blind, deaf, and dumb. And I'm making the same commitment to each of you." (In *Identity* in the "Ready, Set, Grow" series, I describe how I learned these principles from Dr. Sam Chand.)

When we initiated the honesty policy with the staff and board of Oaks Church, we were making a major assumption about each other: that we want God's presence, God's power, and God's wisdom more than we want comfort, clout, and convenience. If that's what we truly want, several things follow:

◆ We'll welcome input from others, even if they don't give it exactly the way we'd like to hear it. Their willingness to be forthright with us is more important than requiring them to dance around our fragile feelings.

- We'll be Spirit-led, not driven by ego or fear. We belong to God. We're His, our church is His, our success is His. We will listen to the Spirit in every decision.
- When we speak the truth in love, we'll let our words be bathed in prayer. We want God to be honored in all we think, say, and do.
- We will do everything possible to work through disagreements to come to unity—not uniformity—but unity. Christ is the head of the Church and of our church. If we aren't in agreement, I'm committed for us to pray and talk until we all get clarity on what God wants us to do.

The last agenda item is the "honesty policy." Before we get up and walk out, I invite people to say whatever is on their hearts. I'll say, "Jesus said He will build His church, and the gates of hell will not prevail against it. This is true, and we can be confident about it as long as we're in unity with Him and each other. The enemy knows he can't defeat us head on, so he is going to try to divide us. As long as we keep our hearts clear with God and each other, we will be unstoppable!"

I look at each person around the table to give each one an opportunity to speak up, to voice any concern, ask any question, or share any offense. We deal with them in the moment, so they won't fester through gossip outside the room.

PAYOFFS

For two main reasons, our honesty policy has been instrumental to the culture of our team and our board. First, we can deal with disagreements, hurt feelings, and concerns immediately so they don't build up. You've seen it, and I've seen it: Someone blows up over a relatively small problem. What happened? A disproportionate emotional reaction is a sure sign there was a lot more under the surface. Like a volcano, the hurt, fear, and resentment had been building pressure, and then, when a seemingly insignificant event happens or a word is spoken—Boom!

Quite often, "The issue isn't the issue." In other words, the problem the person blew up about isn't what's really bothering him. It's something that may have happened days, weeks, or even months before, but it hadn't seen the light of day to be resolved. When we "keep short accounts," we reduce the pressure under the surface. People don't have to spend countless hours thinking about ways to pay people back for the hurt they caused, the magma chamber doesn't build up so there aren't volcanic explosions, and people can genuinely collaborate—and even disagree—without having to win, be defensive, or run when they don't get their way.

When people voice their hurt, anger, or concern, any of several things can happen: They may find out their perception wasn't clear and there wasn't a problem at all. They may discover they didn't have all the facts. Or the other person may apologize, and forgiveness restores unity.

Actually, when leaders first implement this policy, it's common for people to talk about things they've harbored for a long time, and it's messy. If the leader and the group will stay with it, however, the backlog of pent-up emotions subsides, and people can deal with what's currently happening without it being clouded by powerful, unresolved emotions from the past.

A second major benefit of the honesty policy is that the ripple effect of anger is greatly minimized if not eliminated. Before, people walked out of meetings and looked for a sympathetic ear to listen to their complaints. Being "in the know" is a two-edged sword: When we keep influencers in the know, we build unity, but when gossip keeps people in the know, unity is shattered.

For the first few months after we implemented the honesty policy, I ended our board meetings by going around the room asking people if they had anything they wanted to say, but nobody voiced any concerns. Then, one night, when I got to Tom, he swallowed hard and told me, "Pastor, I've noticed the last few weeks in your preaching ... that when the anointing is low, the volume is high."

Now, I swallowed hard. I wanted to tell him, "Tom, when have you ever preached? Do you think you can do better than me?" But thankfully, I took a quick U-turn. Instantly, I realized my response to Tom in this moment would determine if anyone would ever speak up again.

All of this took about five seconds, but to Tom, it probably seemed like hours. I looked at him and said softly, "I think you're right."

He looked stunned. I'm sure he anticipated my defending myself, but instead, I told him, "I've been struggling a lot lately. I've been carrying the weight of fundraising for our building campaign, I've been trying to figure out how we can work with the bank to get the best loans, and I've had some sticky staff issues. Nothing has been going the way I expected. I'm studying more than ever, and I'm praying more than ever. I'm putting in more hours to get ready to preach each week, so it's not a lack of effort. To be honest, I need a breakthrough. I've been in a battle, and I'm determined to keep pressing on. I'm not going backwards. God is going to help me, and I know I'm not going to fail."

I paused to think for a second, and then I continued, "Tom, when I'm on the platform and I'm carrying all this, negative thoughts tell me I'm a failure, and the whole thing is going to fall apart. What you hear as volume is my determination to resist those thoughts and press through it all. But you've helped me see that I need to win the battle privately, so when I'm on the stage, I'll know I've already won. Thank you for your feedback. It's very helpful. I needed to hear it."

At that moment, Tom stood up and said, "Of course that's what's going on! Guys, let's pray for Pastor Scott." With Tom, the rest of the board stood up, walked over to gather around me, and prayed for me. When they were finished, Tom put his hand on my shoulder and said, "Pastor, I'm so sorry. I didn't know what was going on. I shouldn't have said anything."

I replied, "Oh, Tom, you did exactly what you should have done. You spoke the truth because you care about me, and look what happened. Our whole board knows each other a little better, and I feel a lot more encouraged than I did when I came into the room tonight. This was huge for all of us, but especially for me."

You raise the level of others' respect for you if you create a culture where honesty is valued, the backlog of resentments is drained away, addressing problems becomes entirely normal, and present responses are proportionate to the current topic.

It really was huge. Tom's comment helped me see how I was being perceived. My response wasn't defensive, so they realized they really could be honest with me and each other. It gave them more insight into my heart and the pressure I was experiencing, and it brought us together more than almost anything we'd experienced up to that time.

The board members' respect for me rose when I was willing to receive feedback from Tom without being defensive, and my respect for them rose when they loved and supported me in my struggle.

What if Tom had left the meeting and told someone, "Just because Pastor Scott stinks at preaching doesn't mean he has to get so loud!"

That's not at all what happened, and we were all very grateful. It happened because we implemented an honesty policy.

You raise the level of others' respect for you if you create a culture where honesty is valued, the backlog of resentments is drained away, addressing problems becomes entirely normal, and present responses are proportionate to the current topic.

It's important for you to keep your influencers in the know about your plans, but it's just as important for everyone on the team and the board to keep each other in the know about what they're really thinking and feeling.

This principle applies to churches of 100 as much as to those of 10,000, to mom-and-pop stores as much as to those on the S&P 500. It's a concept that values people, treasures honesty, and regularly clears the air so you can focus on what needs to be done in the present.

THINK ABOUT IT:

1) In the past couple of weeks in your organization, what leaders (if any) have poured gas on those they influence to inflame their suspicions and resentments?

2) Who poured water on the fire and put it out?

3) How could keeping the first group in the know have made a difference?

4) Describe the concept of "cascading communication."

5) How can you use this process to get wider, deeper buy-in from every level of leaders in your church?

6) Have you formally invited key influencers to share their observations, critiques, and frustrations with you and with each other? If so, how's it going? If not, why not?

7) What difference would it make for you and your leadership culture if you provided a regular time and place for them to resolve hurt feelings and settle misunderstandings with you and with others on the team and board? What are the risks?

8) What impact would implementing an honesty policy have on your leadership team and board?

Chapter 5

CREATE A ROBUST PROCESS FOR DECISION MAKING

As we've seen, the biggest bomb for a leader isn't making a bad decision. The MOAB, the "mother of all bombs," is making a bad decision without the involvement of key influencers. When a leader makes a bad decision on his own, he's hung out to dry … all alone. But when he takes the time to get the input of his influencers, and together they make a decision, he doesn't lose respect if it goes south. In fact, I'd argue when leaders make decisions on their own without consulting influencers, even if things go well, they lose some respect from their key people because they don't feel valued.

Some read the previous paragraph and insist, "Hey, a bad decision is a bad decision, no matter how it's made." My point is the decision itself is only part of the equation. *How* it's made is just as important, and from my experience, even more. A robust process will at least help you maintain, and hopefully raise, the level of respect your influencers have for you. Let me give you a few examples.

- ◆ When we decided to build a new worship center at Oaks Church, it was a colossal leap of faith. We needed to raise $20 million. I got our board together and told them, "In any large building program, churches hit bumps in the road before it's completed. When this happens to us, I don't want to look around and hear you say, 'Well, Pastor Scott, you got us into this mess, and it's up to you to get us out of it.' There's not going to be an 'I' in this decision. It's only going forward if there's a 'we.'" (I'm so glad I did that because nine months later we hit an unexpected $1 million snag in the project. When the board was informed about the hiccup, they reminded me, "This isn't something you need to carry alone; we're in this together.")

- ◆ In the past year or so, I've spoken on two topics that are flash points in our culture: homosexuality and racial injustice. I was well aware at least some people in the audience would have problems with my positions, so before I spoke, I sent the transcript of my sermons to everyone on the board and key people on our staff team. I was glad to receive their input. Some of them gave me a green light, but a few offered suggestions to clarify, soften, or strengthen particular points. In some cases, I called to ask them to help me reframe the points. Then, when they heard the message, they heard their own words spoken from the platform. Going through this process put water in their buckets, not gas, so when people came up to them after the services to complain or ask questions, they could say, "Yes,

Pastor Scott asked a number of us for input, and we all approved of what he said today. I'm 100 percent behind him." Our board members and key leaders felt included, heard, and valued, and they could represent me and the church to every person in their sphere of influence.

◆ When Jenni and I felt it was time for us to move into the position of global pastors, we were looking at Chris and Cara Railey to be the new lead pastors. I told our board, "This isn't about *me* picking Chris and Cara, and it's not even about *you* vetting them and picking them. We're not moving forward until *God* has given all of us clear direction and confirmation. It's up to Him, not us. If we pick my successor, he may think he has to please us instead of always pleasing God. It's our job to listen to God and do whatever He tells us to do." We fasted and prayed for three weeks, and during that time, I asked each person to trust God to get a vision, a dream, or a word from Him. When we met together at the end of those weeks, I asked each one to stand and share what God had said to him or her. It was crystal clear. We were clapping, shouting, and crying. God had spoken to each of us and through each of us.

◆ The next week, we asked Chris and Cara to be with us on a Sunday, and after the worship service, we all met together for lunch. I had asked each board member and spouse to write their story of how God had spoken to them about the decision, and they publicly read their letters to Chris and Cara. When they finished, each of them hugged Chris and Cara. It took two and a half hours, but nobody was bored, and nobody was in a hurry to leave. It was powerful and beautiful. The only thing left to do was to ask the board members to vote to install Jenni and me and the Raileys in our new roles at our church. Three of the elders were so eager that they tried to make the motion at the same time, and then another three or four yelled out, "Second!" The vote was unanimous. The process was part of God's plan to not just speak to us about a new Lead Pastor but to unite our leadership and give us greater confidence as we moved forward.

A robust process to make wise decisions always includes three key ingredients:
1) Good data,
2) Expert advice, and
3) Buy-in from the key influencers.

GOOD DATA

When I was younger, I assumed I was smart enough to just wing it and come up with a good rationale on the fly for my decisions. That approach didn't last long. I've learned to lean on people who really know their stuff, especially in areas where my training is insufficient (which includes quite a lot). In fact, in many areas, I don't even trust myself to know the right questions to ask.

In a *Forbes* article titled "The Importance of Good Data Quality— Good, Bad or Ugly," Hugo Moreno provides both warnings and encouragement in several areas. He's directly speaking to business leaders, but his points apply to for-profits and nonprofits alike.

◆ Decision making: The better the data quality, the more confidence users will have in the outputs they produce, lowering risk in the outcomes and increasing efficiency. The old "garbage in, garbage out" adage is true, as is its inverse. And when outputs are reliable, guesswork and risk in decision making can be mitigated.

◆ Productivity: Good-quality data allows staff to be more productive. Instead of spending time validating and fixing data errors, they can focus on their core mission.

◆ Reputational damage: Reputational costs range from the small, everyday damage that organizations may not even notice to large public relations disasters. As an example, recall Apple's widely panned Maps rollout in 2012. At the time, it quickly became clear that much of the underlying data was inaccurate or missing, resulting in a product that TechCrunch later called "barely usable."[4]

Here's the process I use to acquire and utilize the best available data:

1) First, I bring my executive team together (or, depending on the size of the organization, two or three of the most trusted leaders) and ask, "What information do we need so we can make a good decision?" (That's an incredibly important but often overlooked question.) I describe the opportunity or the challenge and invite them to ask every conceivable question. If we can figure out all

---

4 Moreno, Hugo. "The Importance Of Data Quality -- Good, Bad Or Ugly." *Forbes*, Forbes Magazine, 5 June 2017, www.forbes.com/sites/forbesinsights/2017/06/05/the-importance-of-data-quality-good-bad-or-ugly/?sh=1705e10b10c4.

the answers, that's great, but if not, I assign one of them to do some research and find the answer.

2) We then meet to write the answers to the questions, for instance:

- What is the goal?
- What's the scope?
- What's the timeline?
- How much will it cost?
- Who will be in charge?
- What are the benchmarks of progress?
- How much of an investment of our leaders' time will it take?
- What's the cost if we don't do it?
- How do we envision success will help us reach our primary mission?

3) When you have these questions (or variations of them) asked and answered, the direction is usually clear. On the other hand, if you don't have these clearly articulated, confusion is inevitable.

> *"The secret to a good meeting is the meeting before the meeting."*

---

4) Hammering out the details of the plan earns the respect of your key influencers. I've learned to create an informative document as a handout, maybe five to ten pages, for a presentation to key stakeholders. Then, when someone asks a question, I can say, "Turn to page three of the handout. That's question #14. Here's what we know, and this is how we'll move forward." If you're

prepared at this level, you'll show that you've thought through everything ... or almost everything, and you have data to support your position. The people in the room quickly become convinced that you aren't winging it at all. You're thorough, you're prepared, and you value them enough to think of the questions they'll ask. Key influencers are impressed, and their confidence in you grows.

EXPERT ADVICE

One of the most important leadership lessons I've ever learned is encapsulated in the title of a book by John Maxwell: "The secret to a good meeting is the meeting before the meeting."[5] The pre-meetings are with people who know more than you do and who are considered experts by the other key influencers. I've already mentioned the fact I always talk to Jack Mourning before we make a move about anything related to construction. He knows everything from zoning and permits to the details of budgeting and building. When I need to make a presentation to our board or the church, I share the vision, and I ask Jack to communicate the specifics and answer any questions. Over the years, our staff, board, and people have learned to trust him. His word is gold.

My legal expertise is only what I've gained by watching courtroom scenes in movies—which is to say, I can speak with very limited insight about murder trials, but on anything else, I'm a blank slate! Legal issues arise from time to time in our church life, and I know

---

5 "Lesson 18: The Secret to a Good Meeting Is the Meeting Before the Meeting." *Leadership Gold*, by John C. Maxwell, Thomas Nelson, 2008.

better than to make any decisions on my own. I always talk to one of our church's attorneys, Tom Davis, Chris Parvin, or Richard Mann. They have legal expertise in different areas, so if I need advice on a contract or a sticky personnel issue, I meet with one of them and ask for their help. When it's time for the board meeting, I either take a written analysis or recommendation from them, or I ask one of them to come to give his input and answer questions.

As you look at your list of key influencers, you'll probably find at least a few who are experts in areas that are vital to your organization.

I also talk to Chad Miles, the CFO for one of the largest home building companies in the DFW Metroplex, about major financial decisions. He's the board treasurer, so he knows our finances inside and out. I meet with him before our board meetings, so we sing from the same song sheet. I don't want to surprise him by bringing up something in the meeting we haven't discussed, and I don't want to say something that he might not agree with and we get into a discussion in front of everyone. If Chad asked hard questions in our board meeting, people would understandably wonder, *Why is he asking those questions? Doesn't he already know? What's going on here?* In our meeting before the meeting, we talk about the issues, and we talk about how to present our recommendations—and they're *our* recommendations, not just mine.

As you look at your list of key influencers, you'll probably find at least a few who are experts in areas that are vital to your organization. Lean on them. Invite them into the earliest stages of exploration and decision making. You undoubtedly have some people who may not have construction, legal, or financial expertise, but they're highly respected among the others on the board and in the church. You'll want to treat them like experts and meet with them before the meeting to inform them, get input, and have a unified voice in the meeting. You want them smiling and nodding when you make your presentation.

In a *Harvard Business Review* article, "How You Make Decisions Is as Important as What You Decide," Laurence Minsky and Julia Tang Peters describe a three-step process to involve experts in critical decisions:

- ◆ Before making a decision at a critical time, I invested time and effort to explore multiple perspectives, needs, and ideas through a proactive dialogue with experts and stakeholders.
- ◆ During the decision making act, I weighed a variety of options.
- ◆ Then, after making the decision, I explained it fully to all stakeholders to reduce the stress of change among those affected.

They conclude:

Note that this inclusive process is not decision making by committee or by consensus. It's the process of constant connection with respected experts and stakeholders, which enables them to recognize business opportunities and threats, and figure out how to adapt or take advantage of them. Habitual outreach prevents insular thinking, opens doors to ideas and collaborative relationships, expands problem-solving perspectives, and increases the range of resources for implementation. Most importantly, it enables real-time adjustments that improve outcomes. This inclusive approach takes 360 degrees of context into account, thereby ensuring better decisions and a higher chance of successful implementation.[6]

Key influencers will drift away (or worse, become antagonists) when they don't feel valued.

Leaning on experts is especially important when you're new to an organization or you're rebuilding credibility after a stumble. It takes some extra time to cultivate these relationships and have multiple meetings with them before the presentation, but it pays huge dividends in smoothing the way forward and raising your level of respect in the eyes of your key influencers. You can borrow their influence until you have more of your own, and then you continue to involve them because they've become valued partners in leading the organization to bigger and better things.

---

6 "How You Make Decisions Is as Important as What You Decide," Laurence Minsky and Julia Tang Peters, *Harvard Business Review*, April 28, 2015, https://hbr.org/2015/04/how-you-make-decisions-is-as-important-as-what-you-decide

BUY-IN

People thrive when they feel valued. Let me put it another way: Key influencers will drift away (or worse, become antagonists) when they don't feel valued. When I sent the transcript of my sermons to the people on our board, it wasn't just a *pro forma* action. I really wanted their input, and I involved them directly by asking them to help me craft the sentences and paragraphs they thought were unclear, too soft, or too harsh.

We can know we've made progress in this area when we go beyond asking them for a thumbs up or thumbs down on our pitch, and we involve them in formulating the pitch. This broadens the base of leadership and turns potential critics into real partners.

Of course, I don't call for a vote by the board until we've had plenty of discussion based on the data we've provided and the input from experts. In fact, I don't call for a vote until I'm sure everyone clearly understands the issues and has shown they've bought in. It's not enough for key influencers to just be okay with the decision; you want them to be as excited about it as you are, and that can't happen unless they want to share the idea with all of the people they influence.

In *Buy-In,* Harvard Business School professor John Kotter writes that getting the support of key leaders is essential to advance real change in business or any organization. He writes:

Buy-in is critical to making any large organizational change happen. Unless you win support for your ideas, from people at all levels of your organization, big ideas never seem to take hold or have the impact you want. Our research has shown that 70% of all organizational change efforts fail, and one reason for this is executives simply don't get enough buy-in, from enough people, for their initiatives and ideas.

Kotter encourages leaders to invite people to push back on an idea or a proposal. He calls this process, "Inviting in the lions." He explains:

If people have no opinions, no objections and no emotions, it usually means they don't care. And you'll be hard-pressed getting their help when you have to actually implement your idea. But conflict shakes people up and gets them to pay attention in a novel way. This gives you the opportunity to say why your idea really is valuable and explain it in a way that wins over hearts and minds—securing their commitment to implementing the solution.[7]

"GOD DECISIONS"

Pastors (and other leaders who are spiritually minded) are tempted to make two bad choices in their style of leadership. (I'm sure there are far more than two, but that's all I'm going to focus on.) First, they give God only a passing glance as they make decisions. They say a perfunctory prayer and decide on their own what they want to do. I

---

7 *Buy-in: Saving Your Good Idea from Getting Shot Down*, by John P. Kotter and Lorne A. Whitehead, Harvard Business Review Press, 2010, pp. 146, flaps.

know exactly how this happens because I've done it so often. I've read a book, listened to a podcast, or attended a conference, and I was captured by an idea. In fact, I couldn't wait to implement it! But that's the point: I needed to wait before the Lord to see if it's what He wanted for our church. Too often, we engage in "motivated reasoning." Our thought processes and goals are already predisposed to come up with a certain answer, so we disregard any opposing data and filter everything through our preconceived justifications. We've already decided before we pray! I'm not saying that great ideas that we gain from outside sources are distractions. They're gifts from God, but we need to unwrap them thoughtfully and prayerfully.

Second, it's vitally important for leaders to hear from God, but hearing from Him doesn't mean you have a pass to skip the process. When you merely announce what you've heard from God to your key influencers, their respect for you may or may not rise. However, you definitely earn respect when you lead them through a process that includes acquiring good data, values expert advice, and involves them in hearing from God so they feel part of the decision.

I get it. We're impatient. After we've heard from God, we're ready to get going. We may have taken weeks or months to come to a conclusion, but we expect our key influencers to be on board instantly. That's not realistic. They need time, too. To build credibility and relationships, we need to add a couple of layers to the process to make it much more robust and effective. Yes, it takes time, but it's more than worth it.

Your job as the leader isn't just to hear from God, but to encourage your top influencers to hear from God so that together you can lead the rest of the people in your organization to hear from Him. Then, the entire community of faith can advance in unity, faith, and boldness.

Don't settle for anything less.

THINK ABOUT IT:

1) Think of the last major decision you faced. On a scale of 0 (zip) to 10 (to the max), how well did you …
   - … gather good data? _____
   - … lean on expert advice? _____
   - … achieve the buy-in of key influencers? _____
   - What did you do well?
   - What could you have done better?

2) Who are some experts you can lean on?
   - What fields do they represent?
   - Are there any glaring holes you need to fill in the experts you rely on? If so, what are they?

3) Think about a major decision you need to make, and write a plan utilizing these components of a robust process:

- With your staff team or key volunteers, think of every question someone might ask. Assign responsibility to find good answers.
- Meet with experts who will give you feedback and participate in the presentation. Borrow their influence.
- Meet with all the key influencers (in roles with titles or not) in "meetings before the meeting."
- Now, with the expert input, write up the Q&A in a document to hand out to your key influencers and for any other presentation.
- In the meeting, give plenty of time for the experts to give their presentations, make recommendations, and answer questions. Give people the handout, and point people to answers. If any significant, unanticipated questions come up, take the time to gather the information and present the answer the next time you meet.
- Always make this meeting an open discussion and invite questions.
- Don't call for a vote until you've given everyone enough time to process the information and buy into the decision. Sometimes this process includes more than one or two meetings before the vote.

Chapter 6

NEVER STOP GROWING

Let me tell a parable about two leaders. (Each one is someone I know, but they will remain nameless.) Richard called me because he was really frustrated. He said, "Scott, I've about had it with the people in our organization … especially our staff and the board. Leading them is like trying to swim holding an anvil. No matter what I do, I get one of two responses: passivity or gripes. I don't know how long I can take this!"

At a conference, I talked to Brett, a business owner I hadn't seen in quite a while. I was glad to see him, and when I asked how his business was going, he erupted in excitement! He told me how he looked forward to every staff meeting and times with the key stakeholders in the business. He went on another 30 minutes talking about all the incredible initiatives they were able to fund to feed hungry children and stop sex trafficking around the world. He said, "The people on our team love working for us because they get more than a paycheck. They get to be a part of something that's making a difference." He finished by saying, "And Scott, they pay me to be part of all this! Isn't that amazing?"

I asked both of them a single question: "Tell me, what's your personal growth plan?"

Richard grimaced and shook his head as he told me, "You've got to be kidding. I don't have time for that. I'm putting out fires from morning 'till night … and way into the night on a lot of days. I can't shoehorn anything else into my schedule. If things were different, I'd make that a priority, but certainly not now. I'm playing catch up all the time."

If a leader is growing, then gifted, passionate leaders are eager to join and contribute, and the organization almost certainly grows.

Brett had a very different response: "It's funny that you should ask. Last year, a friend of mine suggested I create a personal growth strategy, something to sharpen my skills and live a healthier, more meaningful life. I started with a couple of things—listening to pod-casts, reading some great books, and carving out a couple of hours a week to get away to think and pray. I can't tell you how much energy this has given me!"

"You don't have to tell me," I laughed. "I can tell!"

There are many different ways to categorize leaders, but surely one of them is that there are two kinds: those who are committed to personal growth and those who aren't. The differences in their outlooks and their impacts are astounding. The ones who are stretching themselves to grow are usually more optimistic and energetic, and they attract motivated and gifted people. Those who aren't growing are often sour, so they drive off winners and keep all of their whiners.

Leaders like Richard stopped growing as soon as they took their current position, and maybe earlier. They achieved the role they'd always wanted, so their motivation waned. They may have been leaders for 25 years, but they've been stuck in neutral for the last 24. The price they pay isn't just in their lethargy and frustration; they pay a high price in their effectiveness because most key influencers don't respect a leader who isn't growing.

The pattern is clear: If a leader is growing, then gifted, passionate leaders are eager to join and contribute, and the organization almost certainly grows. But if the leader is stagnant, the opposite is true: The very best people steer clear, the organization plateaus, and eventually it declines. When leaders don't devote enough attention to their personal growth, one of two things often happens: Passionate, visionary board members force the leader out and find someone else, or frustrated employees leave to connect with a growing leader, leaving the team with a less-than-stellar cast.

All of us need a personal growth plan, a personal growth team, and clear benchmarks to show our progress toward the goals.

PERSONAL GROWTH PLAN

Most leaders have good intentions about growing and learning. They tell you they're committed to their development in all areas, but very few can point to an actual, written plan. The hard truth is that no one grows because they have good intentions. It takes more than that, and the first step is to craft a workable plan. Let me offer a few suggestions.

1) Find an ally, someone who will help you think through your roles and goals. This person may be a mentor, a life coach, a friend who's growing, or your spouse. This ally needs to be as objective as possible, which means being willing to speak the truth even when you don't want to hear it.

2) List all of your roles: husband or wife, parent, caretaker of your parents, pastor, teacher or preacher, board leader or member, baseball coach, friend, and so on.

3) Evaluate how you're doing in each of these roles. Here's a pro tip: You're probably not doing great in at least one or two of them! Be objective. Face the facts. It's crucial if you're going to make any progress. But also, assess where you're already doing well because you can probably improve in those areas. Ask:

   ◆ What do I need to do to grow?

   ◆ What obstacles need to be overcome so I can grow?

4) Evaluate your current condition in several key areas: spiritually, mentally, physically, financially, and emotionally. For each one,

ask, "What's giving me life, energy, and joy? And where am I falling behind?" And again, ask:

◆ What do I need to do to grow?

◆ What obstacles need to be overcome so I can grow?

5) Write out specific, measurable goals for each role and each key area. Your ally will help you set higher goals (if they're too low) or rein some of them back in (if they're unreasonable).

6) Put your plan into your schedule. If this doesn't happen, all you have is some words on a piece of paper or your laptop. A schedule focuses your attention, limits distractions and excuses, and charts a path for real change.

For instance, here are my goals for the next year:

Key Areas

◆ **Spiritual:** Spend time daily in personal devotions.

◆ **Mental:** Read 12 books and listen to 52 podcasts.

◆ **Physical:** Work out at CrossFit three times a week, lose fifteen pounds.

◆ **Financial:** Give 20 percent, save 20 percent, live on 60 percent.

◆ **Emotional:** Meet with my counselor twice a month.

Key Roles

◆ **Husband:** Take the initiative to connect with Jenni twice a day.

◆ **Dad:** Have a meaningful connection with each of my sons at least weekly; at least once a week, take a creative initiative to do something together: "Let's go ..." "Let's do ..."

- ◆ **Communicator:** Spend plenty of time working on my talks, write them in manuscript form, and get feedback from our team.
- ◆ **Leading leaders:** Engage 12 high-performing leaders of great organizations who want to join my INNER CIRCLE team.
- ◆ **Writer:** Write three books this year.

You'll probably have some of the same key areas, and you may have similar key roles, but your goals may be very different. Expansive goals rarely work because they seem unreachable, so be sure to break them down into bite-sized pieces. For instance, I wanted to lose 15 pounds, so I bought *Calorie Counting for Dummies* and set the weight goal at six months. During that time, I exercised three times a week with my trainer (instead of just one or two times a week before and after I met the goal), and I limited my calorie intake to 1900 a day.

Similarly, if I want to read 12 books this year, I need to read one each month, which means I need to read about 30 minutes a day.

Some of us (I'm looking in the mirror now) are more than a little impatient with the pace of our growth.

Of course, you and your ally need to regularly evaluate your progress and make any mid-course corrections. The need to make adjustments isn't necessarily a character flaw: It's just living in the real world. But it's a genuine character flaw if you fail to even try!

On the next page, there's a look at my weekly schedule that includes time to work toward all my goals.

Every Sunday night, I work on the next week's schedule to be sure I carve out time for the people and activities that help me continue to grow.

Some of us (I'm looking in the mirror now) are more than a little impatient with the pace of our growth. A couple of years ago, I told my counselor I wanted to grow faster in every aspect of my life—and I mean every aspect. He responded, "Scott, I hate to tell you, but it doesn't work that way." He told me a story about a time when he was a little boy, and his parents gave him a coloring book that turns colors when you paint a little water on each section. He didn't want to waste time dabbing water on sections of each page. He wanted the whole book to come alive all at once! He filled the bathtub and dunked the book. The results weren't at all what he was expecting. The pages didn't show vibrant colors. They all mixed together into a dark, dull brown. After he told me his story, he turned to me and said, "Scott, life only works when you work with one page at a time, one section at a time, and one color at a time. If you do, eventually it will look beautiful!"

I get it, but I don't like it. I've learned to set major growth goals each quarter in no more than two key roles. Although I know I need to grow in every role, I focus on the two that I think will double my effectiveness. It's the way of wisdom to identify one meaningful goal in each area, work hard to accomplish it, make it a regular part of

	SUNDAY	MONDAY	TUESDAY
5:00	GET READY	PRAYER	PRAYER
5:30		GET READY	GET READY
6:00	PRAYER	WRITE BOOKS	WRITE BOOKS
6:30			
7:00	TEACHING TEAM	MESSAGE PREP	MESSAGE PREP
7:30			
8:00		TFI STAFF	
8:30			
9:00		RSG STAFF	
9:30			WORK OPEN
10:00	CHURCH: 2 SERVICES		
10:30			
11:00		WORK OPEN	
11:30			
12:00			
12:30			
1:00		LUNCH	LUNCH
1:30			
2:00	LUNCH/REST	WORK OPEN	WORK OPEN
2:30			
3:00		PHONE CALL	PHONE CALL
3:30		PHONE CALL	PHONE CALL
4:00			
4:30		WORKOUT	WORKOUT
5:00			
5:30	OPEN		
6:00			
6:30			
7:00		DINNER FAMILY TIME	DINNER FAMILY TIME
7:30			
8:00			
8:30			
9:00	PREP FOR WEEK AHEAD	PERSONAL TIME TV/ READ	PERSONAL TIME TV/ READ
9:30			
10:00			
10:30			

WEDNESDAY	THURSDAY	FRIDAY	SATURDAY
PRAYER	PRAYER	PRAYER	PRAYER
GET READY	GET READY	GET READY	SABBATH
WRITE BOOKS	WRITE BOOKS	WRITE BOOKS	
MESSAGE PREP/ COMPLETE/ SEND MANUSCRIPT	TWEAK MESSAGE	TWEAK MESSAGE	BREAKFAST W/ JENNI
	PREP ZOOM CALLS	BREAKAST WITH JENNI	READ
		COUNSELING	
	ZOOM CALLS	GOLF	OPEN
LUNCH	LUNCH		
ZOOM CALL PASTOR	ZOOM CALL PASTOR		
WORK OPEN	WORKOUT		
DINNER FAMILY TIME	DINNER FAMILY TIME	DINNER FAMILY TIME	
PERSONAL TIME TV/ READ	PERSONAL TIME TV/ READ	PERSONAL TIME TV/ READ	

our lives, and then move on to the next one. That's the way to make real progress.

PERSONAL GROWTH TEAM

One of the most important steps I've ever taken is to enlist some wonderful people to be on my personal growth team. These people have encouraged me, clarified my direction, challenged me to excel, and supported me through thick and thin. Let me introduce you to them.

Jenni

My wife is my True North. She knows me better than anyone on the planet. She should because we dated for four years before we got married, and we've been married for 30 years (as of this writing). We met when I was 16. She has seen me at my best and my worst. She knows my strengths and my flaws, my hopes and my fears. It has been said of Jesus that He knows the worst about us and loves us still. The same could be said for Jenni's heart for me.

I've learned (sometimes the hard way) that her perspective is more important than any others. For instance, a few years ago, I was asked to join a global leadership organization as a volunteer. I was excited about it, but I knew I often make hasty decisions, so I turned to Jenni. She said wisely, "I'll tell you this, I don't see how you can add anything else to your plate unless you take something off it."

I responded, "Yeah, you're right. I probably won't do it." We decided to pray about it for a week before making the decision.

The next day, I met with my counselor. When I told him about the offer, he advised me to be open to it. I talked to my sons, and they said, "Dad, this is a chance for you to broaden your influence. You should definitely do it!" I called one of my mentors, and he said he'd help me with the transition of addition and subtraction of responsibilities. That night, when Jenni and I were eating dinner, I got a call from the leader of the organization. Of course, he asked if I was taking the role. I told him, "I might. I can see that this is a way to make a difference, so it's hard to say 'no.'"

When I hung up, I looked at Jenni. She wasn't smiling. She raised her eyebrows and said, "Wow, when did 'we' make that decision?"

I knew I was in trouble, so I tried to hedge: "I haven't decided. I mean *we* haven't decided. I talked to a number of people today who encouraged me to lean toward doing it, that's all."

Jenni stared right through me: "So … what other wife did you talk to today?"

She was exactly right. She's my True North, my guiding star, my greatest ally. That means every significant decision runs through her mind and heart, and it always ends with the two of us making the decision together, listening to God's voice, and following His leading to the best of our ability.

It wasn't wrong to talk to the counselor, my sons, and my mentor, but I had given them more clout than Jenni, or at least as much clout for a few hours before my ship was rerouted. I should have told her what they'd said and processed it with her, but to be brutally honest, I didn't mention their comments during dinner because I was afraid she'd disagree with them. (I was right about something at least!) It would have been perfectly fine to tell her about these conversations and ask for her feedback. In the end, that's what happened, but it was a circuitous path to get there. I hope you learn from my mistake. (By the way, you're welcome!)

A Christian counselor

I know some outstanding leaders who get a case of hives when I tell them they should find a counselor. They think going to a counselor is an admission of mental and emotional weakness. They say something like, "I'm not going to a counselor. Do you think I'm nuts?" That's when I tell them I've been going to a counselor every other week for more than 20 years. My counselor is a vital member of my personal growth team. I used to be wary of going to a counselor, as well, but I finally determined that I wanted a professional coach to help me in my marriage, parenting, and pastoring. So, I swallowed my pride and sought out a counselor.

When I started looking for a counselor, I wanted to find someone who was incredibly gifted at counseling and who happened to be a Christian. That's just me. I didn't want someone who was openly skeptical of my faith, but I also didn't want someone who would spout off scripture verses and give me superficial encouragement. I wanted to find someone who was both spiritually astute and clinically sound. And by the way, I decided I didn't want to wait until I was clinically depressed before I made an appointment. I've found that I'm a better husband, father, and leader because I regularly see a wise counselor.

In the last chapter of Galatians, Paul encourages us to "carry one another's burdens" (Galatians 6:2). That's what a counselor does for us. He or she is a professionally trained burden-bearer for the particular weights we carry. Mine helps me untangle my confusing thoughts and process my often conflicting emotions.

Ask your friends for a referral, and even then, if it's not a good fit, find someone else. But don't jump ship because the counselor probes a bit and hits a painful nerve. That's part of the healing process for most of us. Thankfully, I can talk to my counselor about long-buried hurts and current struggles, how to relate to my family and how to be a better leader. Nothing is off the table when I talk to him.

Mentors

Most of us need more than one mentor. In different seasons of life, we need to lean on the insights of particular people who have been through the difficulties we face and can give us wisdom and support. For instance, I've relied on Sam Chand when I've gone through two major transitions in my role as a pastor. I've trusted Jim Sheppard, the CEO of Generis, to help me lead four capital campaigns. Leadership is a lifelong passion for me, and I've learned a lot from John Maxwell,

Gerald Brooks, and Sam Chand, among many others. Pat Springle has assisted me as a writing partner for many years.

But you don't need to wait for a crisis to find someone you trust. You may avoid crises, or at least minimize them, if you have regular connections with people who are further down the road than you in their key roles.

Financial planner
I meet with my financial planner every six months to review our status and adjust our plans for retirement. My goal is to put enough money away so Jenni and I have the flexibility to do anything and everything we sense God is calling us to do, salaried or not. My friend Cal Anderson is an expert in all things financial, and I have implicit trust in his advice.

Health team
I schedule an annual physical to be sure my doctor catches any problems as early as possible, and I have a CrossFit coach who punishes me (not really, but it often feels like it) three times a week. My nutritional goals help me lose weight and avoid junk food. (By the way, barbecue definitely isn't in that category.)

Prayer team
I've enlisted a group of people to pray for me and my family. Every week, I send them my schedule so they can ask God's blessing on the events and meetings. Sometimes they send me scriptures or

encouraging words that came to their minds while they prayed for me. They're always helpful and keep me going.

Teaching team

Over the years, I've seen the need to be more thoughtful and thorough in preparing to communicate. I write out my talks and give the manuscripts to my teaching team at least four days before I speak. Then, the day before I give the talk, I ask them to meet with me and listen as I deliver the talk just to them. They provide valuable input and share how they think people will hear what I'm trying to say.

This process accomplishes several important things:

- It's much better to get honest feedback before I speak than after—when the damage has already been done. As the saying goes: To be forewarned is to be forearmed.
- The run-through the day before is my practice session so the people at the event aren't hearing my first attempt at communicating the content. By the time I actually stand up to deliver the talk, people get my best, carefully crafted message.
- Giving the talk the day before to the teaching team reminds me that I'm talking to individuals, not just a sea of faces. This lets me speak more conversationally, like I'm talking to a small group of friends.

My Personal Growth Team looks like this:

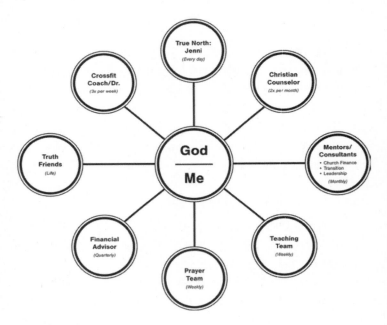

Your growth team may be similar to mine, but your life, your family, and your career may lead you to ask a different set of experts to be on your team. There's no right or wrong. Just find the person who contributes to your development in each key area and role.

GROWTH PLANS

I don't know if this is true for every organization, but I know it was true for me when I led Oaks Church. Part of my role as lead pastor was to help the key influencers on the board construct and accomplish their own growth plans. I knew we would only grow as a church if the key decision makers at the church were growing with me.

One of the greatest gifts you can give to key influencers is to help them develop a growth plan and growth team. You may want to gather two or three of your top leaders and explain what you've been doing to accelerate your personal growth in several areas, and ask them:

- What are some areas the people on our board (and other key influencers) need to grow? (You may need to help them broaden their thinking. Everyone can grow in their family communication, financial decisions, physical fitness and diet, and scheduling. It's helpful for each person to identify strengths and gifts, and then create a plan to sharpen those skills.)
- What undeveloped growth areas are holding us back as a team, a board, and an organization?
- How can we help them craft a plan and construct their growth teams?

Some of your key influencers are probably gifted planners, so they'll thrive on answering these questions and helping you come up with a workable plan. Then, in a staff or board meeting, ask the same set of questions. When our board went through this exercise, we identified three primary goals:

1) Team building: Gain the ability and security to talk honestly with each other, embracing truth and growth over pride and insecurity.

2) Guest services: Analyze what we do well and what needs to improve, and make necessary changes so we can become a terrific service organization.

3) Focus: Clarify our corporate goals so everyone can memorize them, repeat them, and explain them to people who are interested.

To help us reach these goals, I chose three books to inspire us: To build our team, we read *The 5 Dysfunctions of a Team* by Patrick Lencioni; to improve guest services, we read *Raving Fans* by Ken Blanchard and Rick Bowles; and to sharpen our focus, we read *Good to Great* by Jim Collins. I bought copies and gave them one every four months. I assigned specific chapters to read before each meeting. When we met, I taught the main principles from these chapters, and we discussed how to apply the principles in their own lives, their families, and in their work. I also did some homework to identify at least one podcast by a respected leader on the topic, and I sent them a link.

GROWTH PLANS AND TEAMS FOR KEY INFLUENCERS

I would also recommend you share the principles of a growth plan and a growth team and ask the team to come up with their own plans and teams. The reflection process for them is the same as it is for you. I'd print these questions, hand them out, and ask them to share their answers in a subsequent meeting:

Your Growth Plan

1) What are your most important roles?
2) Make an honest assessment of your strengths and needs in each of these roles.
3) What is one specific goal you want to pursue in each one?
4) Who do you need on your personal growth team?
5) In your work, what are the biggest issues that need attention to facilitate growth of your team and your organization?
6) Who do you need on your corporate growth team?
7) What difference will it make to have this plan and this team?

This effort takes time to prepare, and you'll need to devote a portion of every staff or board meeting to the discussion, but it's worth it. The impact on our key leaders has been remarkable. Most of them didn't have a growth plan, and most had never even considered a growth team. This simple approach has had deep and wide benefits to them, their families, and everyone they lead.

And for you, the payoffs of this strategy multiply as you become more focused and determined. You grow in each area that you have a great team to rely on, you're more focused, and the influencers respect you more than ever. Not bad. Not bad at all.

THINK ABOUT IT:

1) List your main roles and begin making an assessment of each one.

2) Who will be your ally? How will this person help you move forward?

3) Write an assessment of how you're doing in the key areas: spiritual, mental, physical, financial, and emotional.

4) Who do you need on your personal growth team? How will you use them?

5) What adjustments do you need to make so that you can grow in each role and each area?

6) What's your growth plan for your key influencers?

7) What is your plan to help your key influencers craft their growth plans and form their growth teams?

Chapter 7

FIX YOUR PROBLEMS

For leaders, there are two unalterable truths:

Truth #1: We all have problems.
I have them, you have them, we all have them. If you're still breathing, you have struggles, setbacks, conflicts, and obstacles. They're a normal part of the human condition.

Truth #2: Your people know you have problems.
Their only question is, "Do you see your problems like I see them?" You lose their respect when they think you aren't aware of your problems, when they're convinced you aren't willing to do anything about them, when they believe you don't have the ability to fix them, or when they suspect you're trying to hide them.

The inability or unwillingness to fix obvious problems is a leak in your leadership bucket, and it's a big hole. Let's look at problems related to buildings, people, and communication.

BUILDING PROBLEMS

When we were raising $20 million to build our new facility at Oaks Church, I was pretty stressed with all the pressure to make it happen. But it wasn't just me: It was the biggest stretch of faith we'd ever taken as a church. One Sunday morning before the services, I walked with one of our board members to the auditorium, and we passed a water fountain with a sign that read, "Out of Order." I thought, *It probably just happened this morning, and it'll be fixed tomorrow.*

But it wasn't. The next Sunday morning, when the board member and I walked to the auditorium, the sign was still on the water fountain. I was really upset. I found Brittany, my assistant, and barked, "Do you see that sign on the water fountain? Take a picture and send it to our maintenance guy. Let him know he needs to fix it immediately … tomorrow morning at the latest!"

My assistant said, "Got it. I'll make it happen, but can I ask you a question?"

"Sure." My blood pressure was gradually returning to triple digits.

She asked, "Why are you so upset about it. It's just one water fountain in the whole church. We have a number of them."

I responded, "You're right, but it's not really about the water. It's about credibility. We're trying to raise $20 million to build a new auditorium. Who wants to give to a new building when we can't take care of the one we have? When we don't fix our problems, we leak credibility."

Key influencers lose respect for you when:

◆ Things aren't clean, especially the bathrooms.

◆ The lawn and landscaping are a mess.

◆ Sounds and smells are unpleasant.

◆ Your car is dirty.

◆ Broken things aren't fixed in a timely manner.

PEOPLE PROBLEMS

Many problems aren't fixed as easily as a water fountain. They're messy, sticky, awkward, and painful—they're problems with people. It's the mean lady who serves as a receptionist, it's the staff member who gossips to friends and forms alliances on the team, it's the board member who isn't really on board with the vision ... The list is endless, but you get the idea.

The people around you lose respect for you when you don't rise to the occasion to fix problems like these. The solutions usually involve some combination of these strategies:

◆ An evaluation process: Have an objective way to assess the impact and attitudes of team members.

- ◆ Feedback channels: Create a system and a culture so people can tell you about their experiences with you, your team, and everything else in the organization.
- ◆ Make the move: Some people have proven to be a negative influence on the team, and they need to be fired. Others have proven they're gifted, but not for their current role, and they need a lateral move. And as the organization has grown, a few people who performed well when it was smaller haven't shown the ability to grow in their skills, and they need to be put in a place where their talents fit the need.

Will people see you as a hard-nosed leader if you implement these strategies? Some will because they don't understand that the roles of a leader are caring for people *and* taking courageous action so the organization is more productive. Remember, some people won't like your strong leadership, but no one, especially your key influencers, value weak leadership.

We don't have to make a choice between compassion and growth. They go hand in hand ... or at least, they *can* go hand in hand. I believe every person in our spheres of influence is a magnificent creation from the hand of God, of infinite value, a masterpiece, a true treasure. These people aren't just a means to accomplish the vision; they *are* the vision. When you have problems with people, it's not like changing a flat tire. They may be difficult, but they're not expendable. Your goal isn't to get rid of them or keep them from annoying you. Your job is to help them discover where they fit best, whether it's in your organization or not. This often means you need to get under the surface, determine the source of the distracting or destructive behavior, and marshal the resources to resolve the underlying problem. Your care has ripple effects throughout the person's life to his or her family, other parts of the organization, and all other relational connections.

Remember, some people won't like your strong leadership, but no one, especially your key influencers, value weak leadership.

Love and leadership are essential. You lose credibility when you don't address and fix the people problems on your board, on your team, and with your volunteers. People are watching, and these leaders represent you. Their attitudes and performances are a direct reflection on you.

Your board, your team, and others who are watching really want you to fix problems with people because those people make everyone uncomfortable and distracted. But they expect you to handle them with kindness and compassion. In other words, they want you to get the receptionist to smile and stop being so mean to people, but they don't want you to say anything that will hurt her feelings!

The way you treat people reveals your heart and your goals like few other aspects of your role as a leader. Take the time and have the heart to do it right.

COMMUNICATION PROBLEMS

I'm sure at least some readers will remember the game when someone whispered a sentence in one person's ear, and each person was supposed to whisper the same thing until everyone in the circle had participated. Quite often, the sentence at the end only vaguely resembled the one at the beginning! This happens every day—often with far fewer laughs—in churches, homes, among friends, and everywhere else with more than two people.

Our public communication errors are quite visible: errors and misspellings on the screen, in handouts and reports, signs that point in the wrong direction, and poorly worded instructions about attending events. These can be solved by taking the extra few minutes to have a fresh pair of eyes look at it.

But private communication is another animal. Here are just a few problems that need to be fixed:

- We say one thing but mean another.
- We hear one thing, but the person meant something else.
- We jump in too early, or we respond too late.
- We speak more than we listen.
- We don't listen at all.

- We depend on digital communication when we could have called or dropped by.
- We react disproportionately to a person or an event, which is a signal something more is going on inside.
- We avoid saying things that need to be said, so the problem festers.

We solve, or at least take steps to solve, problems by establishing a culture where people are regularly invited to give feedback. So, when any of the difficulties on the list (or any others) occur, each person can take the initiative to say, "Just a minute. Let's talk about this."

PROBLEMS YOU CAN'T FIX

When I was the pastor at Oaks Church, we had a problem that couldn't simply be fixed. It was too big and out of our control. All I could do was try to manage it. And as always the key influencers were watching.

Our church is located on I-35E just south of Dallas, but it's far enough south that it's in a rural area between the DFW Metroplex and other smaller cities. Several years ago, a Texas thunderstorm blew through on a Saturday night, and the power at the church went out. We stayed up half the night trying to figure out how to have church the next morning without lights and air conditioning. (I say "we," but I only offered support and frantic prayers. Electricity—not exactly my thing.) A few months later, it happened again, and then again. Over the course of three years, our power was out on Sunday mornings a couple of times each year. It was hard enough to deal with, but when

I checked with other pastors, I always found out that our church was the only one without power. What's that about? I hoped our key influencers didn't find out we were the only losers in the area. Of course, some of them were right in the middle of trying to fix the problem, so they knew.

After the third time it happened, I met with our board and said, "We can't do anything about the weather, but we have to figure out how to solve this." We created a plan: We'd talk to the power company and push them to pinpoint the exact cause of the outage; we considered investing in back-up generators, and we put our best thinkers and most skilled technicians on a task force to fix the problem. The group included a man in our church who works for the power company (We needed an insider.), a highly respected person in the construction business, and some other people who have clout in the community.

The next Sunday morning, I told the church, "I'm so sorry for the inconvenience. Let me tell you what we're doing to manage the situation. We've put a team together to work with the power company to investigate the problem and find a permanent solution. We don't think the problem is with our equipment or wiring, but we're looking at that very closely. We're in talks with executives at the power company, so we're not leaving this with lower or mid-level management. And we're getting bids on generators as a back-up system. I want you to know that we're just as frustrated as you are—and probably much more—but we're on it. Thank you for your patience and prayers. That means more than you can know."

This plan and this announcement didn't fix the power problem, but it went a long way to fix my credibility problem. Our people saw me take action to:

- ◆ Admit the problem was a real headache.
- ◆ Put a team together to focus on this problem.
- ◆ Be very direct with the power company and communicate with its top executives.
- ◆ Explore alternatives.
- ◆ Call people to pray to ask God for wisdom and power—supernatural and literal power!

The problem, we finally realized after the sixth of these events, was that the power lines to our church ran through a golf course. Strong storms knocked limbs off trees, and the limbs were the cause of our outages. I'm not sure why it took so long to isolate the cause, but it did. The power company agreed to trim the trees or move the lines. I didn't care what they did as long as it worked … and it did.

When you can't fix a problem, or the solution will be slow in coming, communicate clearly and often that you're working on it, and you've enlisted others to find a solution. People don't need to respect your skills in electrical engineering, plumbing, professional counseling, or any other major role, but they'll respect you for finding gifted people and getting them involved in fixing the problem.

THINK ABOUT IT:

1) What are building problems you've faced in the past few years?

   ◆ How well did you handle them?

   ◆ What could you have done better to prevent respect from leaking?

2) What are some people problems you've encountered in the last few months?

   ◆ How well did you handle them?

   ◆ What could you have done better to prevent respect from leaking?

3) What are some communication problems you've faced in the past couple of weeks?

   ◆ How well did you handle them?

4) What could you have done better to prevent respect from leaking?

◆ Describe a current problem in one of these three areas (building, people, and communication) that you can't solve, so you have to manage it.

◆ Who are the key influencers who need to get involved from the beginning?

◆ Who should be on the "problem management team"?

◆ How will you communicate that you're handling the problem?

◆ How will this process earn respect from your key influencers and your congregation?

5) Do you have a process to uncover problems you can't easily identify? If so, how well is it working? If not, what would this process look like?

Part 3

Five Ways to Build Relationships

Chapter 8

SPEAK THEIR LANGUAGE

Twenty years ago, when I was voted in as the Lead Pastor at Oaks Church, one of my first calls was to one of the church's key influencers. Tom Davis was an attorney who handled all of our church's legal issues. Everyone respected him, and I wanted to build a good relationship with him. I asked if we could meet for lunch. He answered, "Yes, why don't you meet me downtown at the Dallas Aquarium next Tuesday at noon. I have a membership there, and they have an amazing lunch."

The next Tuesday, I walked into the aquarium. I was nervous because this was an important meeting and I didn't want to blow it, but I was optimistic that we'd connect. We'd gotten to know each other only superficially when I was the youth pastor and my dad's associate pastor. Now it was time to take a big step in our relationship.

Tom met me at the desk, and he said, "Before lunch, let me show you around." He took me to his favorite exhibits on the first floor, and he arranged for me to have access to every exhibit after we had lunch.

We walked back to the restaurant and were escorted to our table. After we ordered, I told Tom my ideas about plans I was going to present at the next board meeting. I asked questions about the upcoming property purchase and the next steps in construction, and I asked for his input on the capital campaign that we were launching. It was a very pleasant and informative conversation. Before we left, I told him, "Tom, this is a big transition for me, for the church, and for everybody involved. I want to grow into the role as the lead pastor, and I want to lean on all of your expertise in contracts and all the other legal matters. I respect you, and I value your contribution to me and the church. I'd like to meet with you once or twice a month to talk through things before board meetings. I want to be sure I have all the information from you, so my presentations will be wise and thorough. And besides that, I'd like to know you better and grow in our friendship."

Tom smiled as he told me, "Pastor, I'm committed to help the church in any way I can. I'll look over any documents you email me, and I'll give you feedback on any agenda items before each board meeting. But I don't have time to meet with you twice a month—or even once a month. I'm honored that you want us to be better friends, but I don't have time for that right now. I hope that doesn't hurt your feelings."

Hurt my feelings? Who, me? I laughed (or at least it was supposed to be a laugh) and told him, "Oh, no. That's perfectly fine. I completely understand. I really appreciate all the help you give. You're very generous in every way."

We got up, walked to the front of the restaurant, shook hands, and parted ways. On the way to the car, I felt totally mortified. Among many other thoughts, these coursed through my mind: *What just happened? What did I say that offended him? Hurt my feelings? Yeah, more like crushed them! Why did he agree to have lunch with me if he doesn't want a relationship?*

When I got home that night, I unloaded all my disappointment on Jenni. She listened very carefully, and then she said, "Scott, Tom wasn't being rude. He's not resistant to the vision of the church, and he doesn't dislike you. His response wasn't a personal attack. He respects you, and he cares about the church. If you remember, he believed in you and supported you to be the new lead pastor." (Hmmm. She made a good point … a really good point.)

Jenni wasn't finished reorienting my perspective: "Look at all Tom does for the church. He's not backing away. He told you that he'll help in any way he can. He gives hours to come to the board meetings, he teaches a Sunday school class every week, and he handles all the legal work for the church. Scott, he's one of your biggest fans! And besides, he wouldn't have taken you on a tour of the Aquarium and given you a full-access pass if he was pushing you away. It sounds like the way he expresses love and appreciation is different from yours, and today, you didn't speak his language. He communicates love through tangible gifts and service ... and he speaks these really well!"

As usual, Jenni had far more insight than I did. I realized I needed some kind of framework to help me understand what makes people tick. If I can't identify what motivates them, I won't be able to lead them well.

CHOCOLATE, STRAWBERRY, AND VANILLA

News flash: A lot of people aren't like me! (Actually, I still have a problem believing this statement, but I know it's true.) Psychologists and other experts have produced dozens, if not hundreds, of models to identify and describe patterns of how people are motivated and how they relate to each other. Most of us are familiar with the DiSC profiles (dominance, influence, steadiness, and conscientiousness), the Myers-Briggs Type Indicators (identifying 16 main types), the Enneagram, the Birkman Method, and plenty of others. All of these can be very helpful to individuals, couples, and teams because they offer objective appraisals of how people think, feel, and act differently to similar situations.

One of the most popular tools to help us understand other people is Dr. Gary Chapman's book, *The 5 Love Languages*. He observes people are touched emotionally by different expressions of esteem and affection. When we speak a person's "love language," it's speaking French to someone from Paris, Swahili to someone from Kenya, Spanish to a person from Madrid, and Portuguese to someone who flew in from Rio. No translation is needed; they get it, and it makes them feel understood and valued. Chapman's five "languages" are words of affirmation, acts of service, gifts, quality time, and physical touch. These are spread fairly evenly among the population, with words of affirmation more common than the others.

> ### *If I can't identify what motivates them,*
> ### *I won't be able to lead them well.*

I've tried hard to recognize the love languages of the people around me, but I often view them through my own prism. I remember walking up to Jenni, patting her on the bottom (Is that too much information?) and whispering, "Looking hot today, Babe."

She turned to look at me, rolled her eyes, and said, "Sorry, no speaka dat language, amigo," which translated means, "Honey, try to remember that you speak words of affirmation and physical touch, but I speak acts of service and quality time. So … after you take out the trash, let's brew some tea, sit together, and talk."

Thanks to Jenni, I realized I'd tried to speak my love language to Tom when we went to lunch. No, I didn't grope him and call him "honey," but I didn't first discover his language so I could speak it. Because I assumed we spoke the same language, I completely misunderstood his communication.

TRY THIS

How can you find out what really motivates people? And how can you learn what revs their engines? No matter which personality model you prefer, or if you prefer none at all, let me make some suggestions to help you understand people and make better connections with them.

Ask open questions

Closed questions have a definite answer: "What time is it?" There's not a lot of self-disclosure when the person says, "10:30." There are times when these are exactly the right kind of question to ask, but not when you want to understand what's going on in a person's heart and mind.

Limiting questions have a definite answer, often "yes" or "no," but they come across as a test instead of open dialogue. I might ask, "Can you fix that?" or "Will you pick me up?" These questions may reach for a bit of information, such as, "Who went with you to the meeting?" Or they can ask for the reason a person made a particular choice, like, "Why did you do that?" Depending on the level of trust in the relationship, these questions can come across as judgmental.

Open questions don't have a particular answer, and if they do, they provide the person with a way to explain his or her response. They often explore the person's desires and logic, and they often begin with "how," "why," or "what if?"

As an exercise, notice the questions you ask for the next couple of days, and determine which ones are closed, limiting, and open. Make a point of using "how," "why," or "what if?" in your conversations. And if you need to ask a closed or limiting question, follow it up with an open one. Of course, there are times you need information, and you don't want to spend time listening to people share their hearts about it! But we show we care by asking open questions ... and then listening to the answers.

Listen

Really listen. When our spouse, kids, or co-workers are talking, how much of the time are we thinking about what we want to say, how we'll refute the person's point, or about something we'll be doing after this boring conversation? Do you think people notice when we're not tracking with them? Yeah, they do.

Active listening is a skill all of us can develop, and it's really not that hard. Here are a few tips:

- ◆ Pay attention.

Pay attention to the person's words and body language, and notice any disconnect between the words and the tone of voice, facial expressions, or posture. But also, pay attention to yourself. Are you drifting off and thinking about something else? When this happens (and it will), bring yourself back to the conversation.

◆ Reflect.

Mirror the person's words and feelings. You might say, "This is what I hear you saying …" or "You feel hurt, don't you?" It's amazing how seldom we do this, and it's equally amazing how powerful it is. But don't do this so often that it comes across as a canned approach. A good rule of thumb is this: In every significant conversation, reflect at least once, but not more than twice.

We need to provide opportunities for them to tell their stories, either in a group setting or one on one.

◆ Go a little deeper.

I know I'm really listening to Jenni or anyone else if I'm asking second and third questions. These tell me (and more importantly, they tell them) that I'm engaged, I'm not in a hurry to get this over, and I really care. One of the very best statements in any conversation is simply, "Tell me more about that."

◆ Confirm the message.

Near the end of a meaningful conversation, provide confirmation that you've heard, you've understood, and you appreciate the person's honesty.

Connect the dots

When Jenni and I were dating, every piece of information was new. It was thrilling (for me, anyway). Gradually, the painting of our relationship began to take shape. I understood more of what gave her a shot of enthusiasm and what bored her, the topics that brought out lots of details and the ones that she blew by pretty quickly, and the people and events that elicited deep emotions and those that were "meh." If our conversations had been one of those children's books with dots to connect to draw a horse, I was glad to have a pencil in my hand! I was highly motivated to understand as much about Jenni as I could. As I've mentioned, I'm still learning … and I always will be.

In our relationships with key influencers, we need to connect the dots. We need to provide opportunities for them to tell their stories, either in a group setting or one-on-one. And as they tell us about themselves, we ask open questions, we really listen, and we connect the dots from the past to the present.

CLUELESS

When Chris Railey came back to our church to become the lead pastor, we'd been close friends for 13 years, but I had never tried to identify his love language. I assumed he was just like me. Clueless, yeah, I know. Totally clueless. So I asked him, and he told me gifts communicate love and appreciation to him. At that moment, the lights came on. I realized as the Director of Church Multiplication Network, he had produced hoodies, jackets, and hats to give to people involved in the ministry.

When his birthday approached, I had an idea. We work out together at CrossFit, but I noticed he didn't have a pair of CrossFit shoes. I found the very best shoes in the colors and the design I thought he'd like. And get this: I bought them and wrapped them myself. I didn't even ask Jenni to do it for me. We had Chris and his family over for a surprise birthday party, and I gave them to him. He seemed equally surprised and excited. He wore them the next day when we worked out, and a week later, he sent me a picture of them and a text: "I can't believe you bought me these shoes!"

I've talked to a lot of people who have told me the people closest to them—spouse, parents, children, and best friends—haven't cared enough to find out what communicates love to them. One man told me that neither of his parents "get" him. He said sadly, "You'd think they'd have noticed that I really don't care about all the money and stuff they've given me over the years. What I want is time with them, not their things."

"Maybe they couldn't give themselves," I offered.

"Or maybe they didn't care enough to notice," he instantly replied.

TALK TO ME

At one point, I gathered our key influencers and gave a talk about the five love languages. I told them how I've tried to speak my language to Jenni, but we're from different lands. But I also could tell them I'm doing better, making progress in learning her language and speaking it—maybe not fluently, but at least adequately. I gave them a handout with the five love languages and some descriptions of each one, and I gave them an exercise: Pair up, share their primary and secondary love languages, and identify their spouse's primary love language.

I gave them plenty of time. The place sounded like a sawmill at full tilt. Obviously, they were really getting into this! After a while, we got back together, and I asked each one to tell us what they'd learned about the other person. I also asked them to tell us one or two ways they could speak that person's love language. Each one, too, shared his spouse's love language. I took notes like my life depended on it! These guys were giving me more information about their hearts than I'd ever heard, and it was just one simple exercise in a single meeting. I made careful notes of how each one felt loved and valued. This was a gold mine for me.

The Golden Rule is as follows: "Do unto others as you would have them do unto you." How do you want people to treat you? You want them to take the time to get to know you, listen to you, connect the dots of your life (maybe better than you ever have), and give you affection and honor in the way that taps into your heart. And that's how you need to treat them, too.

By the way, Tom Davis has been a faithful, gracious, and generous leader in our church for over four decades. I don't know where we'd be today without his wisdom and hard work. No, we haven't had a lot of lunches together since the one at the aquarium, but thanks to Jenni showing me that people are very different, Tom and I haven't needed to have frequent lunches to appreciate each other.

Every key influencer in your organization has a particular personality, specific desires and expectations in relationships, and ways they feel loved and honored. If you take time to know them and find out how to communicate, "I appreciate you," you won't hear them say, "You no speaka me language."

THINK ABOUT IT:

1) What do people say and do that makes you feel valued?

   ◆ What do they say and do that shows they mean well but doesn't connect with you?

2) Think of how you interact with one person: your spouse or a key influencer. On a scale of 0 (I'm terrible at this!) and 10 (Watch me work!), rate how well you:

   ◆ Ask great questions _____

   ◆ Actively listen _____

   ◆ Connect the dots _____

◆ What does this analysis tell you about how well you're connecting with this person's heart?

3) As you think about the same person, write a plan to do one thing in the next meaningful conversation to:

◆ Ask great questions:

◆ Practice active listening:

◆ Connect the dots:

◆ (Review these sections of the chapter to give you ideas.)

4) What are some ways these practices can become habits in your conversations with your family and key influencers?

◆ What difference will it make ... to you and to them?

Chapter 9

WHEN YOU REMEMBER ...

More times than I can count, I've walked into our house and found Jenni and a man talking in the kitchen, the bathroom, or somewhere else in the house. They're plumbers, electricians, cable installers, or some other technician who has come to do some work on our house, but they got much more than they imagined. They found a friend. I've told Jenni that she must have a neon flashing sign on her forehead that's visible to these guys: "I care about you. I *really* care!" These guys stay twice as long as they need to. When I come in, they're often standing with their wallets open showing Jenni pictures of their wife and kids. I can overhear them before I walk into the room. They're talking about a new baby, their last vacation, a nagging health issue, their parents, their hopes and dreams, what they had for breakfast, and everything else imaginable.

If one of them comes back to finish a job, or comes back a year later to do something else at our house, Jenni not only remembers their names and faces—she remembers their kids names and how they're doing in school, the joys and struggles they've shared with her, and other details of their lives. She asks how his mom's surgery went, if his daughter is still dating that guy, how the dog that was hit by a car is doing, and if the promotion finally happened. Invariably, she tells each one, "I've been praying for you. What has God done since I saw you?"

Jenni has incredible chemistry with these people, and sometimes I get impatient for them to leave. When I've made subtle hints that they've finished and it's time to go, they don't even acknowledge what I've said. They're completely absorbed in talking with Jenni. And many of these guys aren't what you'd call natural conversationalists. They spend all day every day under sinks, in the attic, or wrestling with toilets. Sometimes when they're in the neighborhood on another job, they knock on our door to tell Jenni about something she promised she'd pray about. These people consider Jenni to be a trusted, valued friend … because that's how she treats them.

One time when Jenni and I met with our counselor, I told him that I'm amazed that these guys open their hearts so often and so widely to her. He responded in a way that surprised me: "That makes me so sad."

I nodded and told him, "I know! It takes me forever to get them out of our house!"

He shook his head. "No, Scott. I'm not talking about that. It's sad that people are so lonely, so desperate to have someone care about them. When Jenni connects with them at a heart level and expresses how glad she is to see them, they soak up her genuine kindness. When most people ask, 'How are you doing?' it doesn't mean anything, but when she asks the question, they sense she really wants to know ... and she isn't in a hurry for them to do their work and leave. When they begin to actually tell her how they're doing, their hearts are moved by her obvious love. Scott, 90 percent of the people around us don't have anyone who cares enough to really listen to them."

FLIP THE SWITCH

I'm a leader, and leaders are communicators. We're visionaries, planners, and motivators who need to be at least one step ahead of our people. That means we've already spent a lot of time thinking about every topic we bring up to our staff and board. The sign on my forehead has a different message than Jenni's; it's "Just push play." All it takes is one question, and I'm in full motormouth mode. Actually, I don't need a question to launch a barrage of my verbal rockets.

When I was a youth pastor, I spent some time with Jeanne Mayo, who was and still is a legend in youth ministry. I spent an hour and a half with her, and I talked nonstop. I told her what we were doing in our ministry, our plans for the future, and my frustrations. She smiled and occasionally interjected, "That's so good, Scott." At the end of our time, we hugged and left. Suddenly it dawned on me I'd been sitting with one of the most brilliant ministry minds in the world, and

I hadn't let her say more than a few words. I had tried to impress her with what we were doing, but our ministry was probably less than a tenth of what God was doing through her. I had completely blown the opportunity to tap into her wisdom.

Over the years, I've learned something: One of the dumbest, most unproductive things leaders (like me) do when they want to build relationships with key influencers is dominate the conversation. It's easy to talk non-stop about ourselves, our vision for our organization, and our plans to get there. Don't key influencers want to know those things? Don't they need to know? Yes, but they also need something else—to know we value them, and we communicate that by shutting up and listening. When I was younger, I was sure that the way to impress key leaders was to explain my vision over and over and talk about all of my achievements. That impressed them alright … it impressed them that I cared far more about me than them.

For a long time, I've been learning—and I'm still in the process of learning more—to ask great questions, to invite people to tell me their life's story, their hopes, their fears, their successes, and the things they'd love to do over. I want to move beyond facts to their motivations. I look for cues of changes in their tone of voice, and I sense where an untapped well of emotions might be. I can sense that they're often surprised by my interest, especially when I ask follow-up questions or say, "That's amazing! Tell me more about that." Later, I've found out some of them told their friends, "I really enjoyed talking with Scott. He's really sharp!" Which is really funny because all I did was ask questions and listen. People are most impressed when others truly value them with no strings attached. I've learned some very important lessons from Jenni, and that's made all the difference.

One of the dumbest, most unproductive things leaders (like me) do when they want to build relationships with key influencers is dominate the conversation.

GET PERSONAL

If all we talk about is success or failure, and all we analyze is how to be more productive, people soon conclude that the only thing that really matters to us is our personal and organizational success. To lead people well, they need to know we care about them. We're shepherds *and* visionaries—not one or the other. It doesn't take a PhD to figure out what matters most to people:

- If they're married, ask about their spouse, and not just superficial facts. Ask about their story: how they met, their first years of marriage, what they enjoy about each other, where they go on vacation, and other questions that get to the heart.

- If they have kids, ask about them: their personalities, which parent they're like and not like, what they love to do, their triumphs and struggles.

- If they're on your team or are key influencers, ask about when they feel most fulfilled, when they feel frustrated in their work, and where they see themselves in five or 10 years.

And as I mentioned in the last chapter, don't spend your time thinking about the next thing you want to say while they're talking. Pay attention, ask follow-up questions, and reflect what's said and felt.

It's very clear: The extent we engage people on a personal level is the ceiling of our relationship and our influence with them. The point is this: Raise the ceiling by getting personal with them. But there's another factor that connects us with them more deeply … far more deeply. It's remembering what they told us.

REMEMBER WHAT THEY SAY

When I see someone months after we've talked about something important, and they don't even remember, I wonder if the person really values me. But if this person says, "Hey, Scott, what happened with your son and his girlfriend?" or "How did you handle that problem you told me about?" or "Tell me again about the time you tripped when you were walking up to the platform on Sunday morning," I feel understood and valued.

Again, Jenni is the master at remembering. Actually, I kind of resent it because it's second nature to her—she doesn't even have to try! But I have to try, and try hard. To be honest, I've had to create a system to serve as my AI, artificial intelligence.

A few people—a very few people—can remember almost everything that has happened to them. In a *Smithsonian* article, Randy Rieland reports:

At last count, at least 33 people in the world could tell you what they ate for breakfast, lunch and dinner, on February 20, 1998. Or who they talked to on October 28, 1986. Pick any date and they can pull from their memory the most prosaic details of that thin slice of their personal history.

Others, no doubt, have this remarkable ability, but so far only those 33 have been confirmed by scientific research. The most famous is probably actress Marilu Henner, who showed off her stunning recall of autobiographical minutiae on "60 Minutes" a few years ago.

What makes this condition, known as hyperthymesia, so fascinating is that it's so selective. These are not savants who can rattle off long strings of numbers, Rainman-style, or effortlessly retrieve tidbits from a deep vault of historical facts. In fact, they generally perform no better on standard memory tests than the rest of us.[8]

In case you didn't know, my name isn't on the list of these 33 people— but it doesn't matter because these people can only remember what happened to them, not to other people they've known. Like me, they have to work at remembering facts and emotions about other people. When I'm talking with people and asking them to tell me their stories, I take notes. If they ask what I'm writing, I'm really clever. I tell them, "I'm taking notes, so I can remember your story." Pretty shrewd, huh?

8 "Rare People Who Remember Everything," Randy Rieland, *Smithsonian*, September 4, 2012, https://www.smithsonianmag.com/innovation/rare-people-who-remember-everything-24631448/

When we finish talking, I write the main points in the contacts section of my phone. This may include prayer requests, an upcoming decision, a difficulty, a funny story, or a family problem. Whatever it is, I write it in my phone. If it's important enough for them to tell me about it, it's important for me to remember it.

> *Sometimes, I meet someone who wouldn't normally stay on my radar, but I sense God has put us together for something special.*

Then, the next time we talk, I open the page and I have all the information right in front of me. I can pick up our previous conversation like we'd talked only an hour before. It often amazes them—and it always amazes me that it means so much to them. In that moment, what conclusions do they draw? That I really care about them, that I've really listened and understood, and they must be really important to me.

These conclusions are true, but it's not my natural or spiritual gifting to remember details of people's lives, so I've had to create a structure to help me. Jenni does it effortlessly, but I have to be intentional and disciplined to prod my memory. I really do love people, and this system gives me a way to show it.

To be honest, I don't have these entries about everybody I meet. That would be overwhelming. I've prioritized my key influencers and key contacts in our community and around the country (and some in other countries), but when in doubt, I include the person. Remembering details and emotions shows love in a way that can't be measured. When I can talk about those things, the sign on my forehead flashes, "You matter to me! I really care about you!" But if I don't remember, I'm signaling, "I want you to think I care about you, but I'm not willing to do the work to keep up with what's on your heart." (Yeah, that's too long for a forehead sign, but you get the idea.)

YOU NEVER KNOW

I'm honored to meet thousands of people every year—people who come to our church, people I meet at events, and people I see wherever I go. Sometimes, I meet someone who wouldn't normally stay on my radar, but I sense God has put us together for something special. Not long ago, I was invited to attend a small gathering of leaders from different fields. The hosts invited me to come a day early and have dinner with them. When I sat down, someone took the initiative to make all the introductions at our table. As he went around, he introduced me to a man sitting near me: "Scott, this is Charlie Bollinger. We call him 'the deer apostle.'"

I felt like I was the only one not in on the joke, so I bit: "Deer apostle, huh? What's that about?"

The man making the introductions laughed and said, "He's got the most amazing deer lease on the planet! People come from all over the world to hunt with him."

"That's awesome," I remarked. "That's a new one for me." For the rest of the night, I asked Charlie to tell me all about his lease, the huge deer with gigantic antlers they've killed, and the people who have hunted with him. I also discovered a deep passion for God and an amazingly generous heart.

Somewhere between the first and last bites of dessert, Charlie told me how much he and his wife love the CCM artist, Toby Mac. I said, "My daughter-in-law, Holly, sang with Toby Mac. They're close friends."

Charlie almost dropped his fork. "You've got to be kidding! That's amazing! I'm so glad we sat together tonight. Please give me your contact information. I want to stay in touch."

"I'd love that." We swapped our email addresses and phone numbers. I had a hunch this wasn't the end of our connection.

As soon as we left the table, I pulled out my phone, started a new contact, and wrote his name, "deer apostle," wife: Sheila, son: Trey, loves Toby Mac … great guy!

About two months later, my phone buzzed in my pocket. It was Charlie, and instantly, all of his information came up on my phone. I answered, "Hey, deer apostle! What's going on?"

He asked, "How did you remember what people call me?"

I laughed and said, "How could I forget that?" (Well, you know how I couldn't forget.) "How's Sheila? Is she feeling better?"

"Yes," he told me. "She's doing much better. Thanks for asking. That means a lot."

"And how's Trey?"

"Yes, he's doing well ... in fact, really well. I'm really proud of him. Thanks for asking." He paused for a second, and then said, "Scott, I'm calling to see if you can swing some tickets for me to a Toby Mac concert ... and if there's any way to meet him, Sheila and I would love that!"

I'm so glad I had taken the one or two minutes to put the information about Charlie in my phone. It made a world of difference. Would I have remembered his nickname? Probably. Would I have remembered Sheila's health problem? Maybe, maybe not. Would I have remembered Trey? Not a chance.

Every time my phone rings, I have instant reminders of what's important to the person on the other phone. But I hate it when I forget to take that minute to write down the information, and I can't remember what's going on in the person's life. I've missed a golden opportunity to remember details, value the person, and build a stronger, deeper relationship.

A detail doesn't have to be a cataclysmic event in the person's life. It can be something as simple as spilling a drink on his wife at a restaurant or running over his son's tricycle. More than once, I've asked, "How's the new puppy doing? Many messes in the house?" No, the topic isn't very important, but the fact that I remembered certainly is.

My best efforts to connect with people beyond the superficial level aren't as good as Jenni's normal, everyday interactions with friends and strangers, but I'm making progress.

I wish I were more like Jenni, but I'm not. It's not a tragic flaw; it's just that I need to try a little harder to show I care. For you, whether it's second nature or intentional, remembering other people's stories— family names, funny things, hopes, and fears—really matters to them. It opens doors, cements friendships, and shines a ray of light into that person's heart.

When I told a friend about this habit, he asked, "Why don't more leaders and more people do something like this? It seems to be really helpful."

I thought about it for a while, and I told him, "That's a great question. I think there are several reasons: First, they've never thought of anything like writing things down, so they can bring up the information when they need it. It's not even a concept to them. Second, if they hear about the idea, they may think it's too much trouble to spend a minute jotting down the information. Third, they assume they'll remember next time (but they probably won't). And maybe fourth, their model of leadership leans hard toward giving direction and away from forming friendships, so they don't see the value in it."

He asked, "When they learn about this idea, do you think they'll give it a shot?"

"We'll see," I told him. "I sure hope so. It's done wonders for me. I'm reaping the compound interest of loving people for a long time—and living with a woman who is by far the most genuine, caring, compassionate person I've ever known. My best efforts to connect with people beyond the superficial level aren't as good as Jenni's normal, everyday interactions with friends and strangers, but I'm making progress. For me, it doesn't just happen. It's intentional."

Like any habit, this one requires practice. At first, you might remember to write the information half of the time. That's great! It's far better than before. And as you keep going, you'll see the amazing impact of being able to talk about things that matter when you see or talk to people again. The look in their eyes will motivate you, and soon, you'll be sure to take notes so you don't miss a thing. Of course, you'll blow it from time to time. Don't worry about that. Just keep moving forward, so you can touch the hearts of the people you meet.

Whatever it takes, do it.

THINK ABOUT IT:

1) Who do you know whose sign on their forehead flashes, "I really care about you!" What impact does that person have on others … and on you?

2) What sign would your spouse say is flashing on your forehead?

   ◆ What would your kids say?

   ◆ Your staff?

   ◆ Your board?

3) How well do you explore the details of people's lives? If you do it well, what has prompted your interest? If you don't do it so well, what are your preoccupations?

4) How would having a system for remembering names and details of stories help you build better relationships with your key influencers?

5) Make a list of your ten key influencers and write down some details of the "stories of their hearts."

6) Enter these in your phone and bring up at least one point the next time you talk to each one.

7) With at least one person in the next 24 hours, say, "I'm interested … would you tell me your story?" And at least once when the person assumes you've heard enough, say, "Tell me more about that." Observe what happens in you, in that person, and in the relationship. Then write it in the contacts on your phone.

Chapter 10

VALUE THE PEOPLE THEY VALUE

If we don't value what key influencers value, they won't feel understood, and they won't feel appreciated. What do the vast majority of them value more than anything else? Their families.

It works both ways. Several years ago, I interviewed a man for a key position on our staff team. We went to a restaurant for dinner, and I invited Jenni, Dillon, and Hunter to come along. I asked the guy the normal questions I always ask people to find out more about them, their experiences, and their dreams for the future. And of course, we talked about the specific responsibilities of the job. After we finished and we were walking to the car, Dillon asked, "What do you think, Dad? Are you going to hire him?"

I started to answer, but Jenni jumped in, "I can answer that."

I laughed and asked, "Really? You already know? And you're sure, are you? Do you have some secret information I missed?"

The boys chimed in to rag on their mom, "Yeah, Mom. How do you know?"

She announced to them, "There's no way in a million years your dad would hire that guy for such a high-level position at the church!"

Rich, real, lasting connections are made when we treasure what means the most to another person.

I was only mildly surprised. I was well aware that she often has far more insight than I do when we talk to people. I just said, "Okay, what did you see?"

She turned to me and said, "He doesn't know how to value people. From the minute we sat down, he looked at you the whole time. He focused on you, talked to you, and listened only to you. He never said a word to me or the boys. He never even looked over and nodded to us. That tells me he has no concept of what matters most to people. He doesn't know how to connect. And he obviously doesn't value what you value, because you value us!" She looked at the boys and told them plainly, "Your dad certainly wouldn't hire someone like that!"

By now we were standing next to the car. Dillon turned his gaze from his mom to me. He didn't have to say a word. I told him, "Son, you have a very wise mother!"

He then asked, "Dad, did you see that, too?"

"Absolutely. I appreciate eye contact, but he only gave eye contact to me. It was, to be honest, incredibly rude to your mom, your brother, and you. I'm not going to hire a person for a pastoral role who doesn't value my wife and my sons. That's not just about leadership; it's about the value of relationships."

Dillon asked, "But Dad, couldn't you teach him? Can't he learn to value people?"

"Yes, that's possible," I told him, "but he's 43 years old. If he doesn't understand people better by this point in his life, he either hasn't been sharp enough in people skills to get it, or he really doesn't care about people. Either way, he doesn't fit our culture." I paused for a second or two and then said, "Son, I'm more than happy to teach some skills, but this is a matter of the heart. Do you understand?"

He nodded. "Got it."

To build stronger relationships with key influencers, we've looked at the importance of listening, and we've addressed the power of remembering facts about people. In this chapter, we'll dive a little deeper. If we never mention a person's family and ask about their hopes and dreams, the relationship remains focused on performance and goals. Rich, real, lasting connections are made when we treasure what means the most to another person.

Let me offer some ideas you might want to use.

KNOW THEM BY NAME

When John Maxwell speaks at events, people often ask if they can take their picture with him. They want to be identified with him and show their friends they have a connection. But in some cases, John flips the script and asks people if he can take a picture with them, so he can keep their image to remind him of them. People are usually equally astonished and honored. John puts these photos in his contacts and includes other information, so he can remember details when he talks to them again.

As I've made this a habit, it has helped me remember facts, dates, and events in the lives of people I know, and the look on their faces tells me they feel honored that I'd take the initiative to take their picture.

But the goal isn't to have a bunch of pictures on my phone. I use the pictures to recall names and stories. Nothing sounds better than for someone to call you by name. It tells you that you're important. If you're the leader of hundreds or thousands, it's a really big deal when you remember the names of people beyond your normal circle of contacts. I also use these pictures to send personalized cards. I use an app on my iPad called *Felt* to make a postcard out of the picture. The app is amazing. I put the picture on the postcard and then take my Apple Pencil and write a personal note on the back about our time together. I then put the person's address in the app, and *Felt* sends it out for me. It only costs a few dollars to value people in a personal and creative way.

BE PREPARED

When I'm going to have a phone, Zoom, or in-person meeting, I look at the person's contact information in my phone, so I'll be ready. I may jot down some cryptic lines to guide my conversation, or I just have the contact open on my phone. I ask about any concern or opportunity we discussed when we talked previously.

I ask about the spouse. Recently I told a friend, "How's Shaylyn? I hope she's feeling better. Tell her Jenni and I said 'Hi!' We love her so much. She's amazing. I appreciate her thoughtfulness, especially toward Jenni. You may not know this, but she sent Jenni a beautiful card a few weeks ago. She was really touched by it. Both of you mean a lot to us."

I ask about the children and, if there are any, the grandchildren. If you heard last time about a son excelling in sports, ask how he's doing. If you heard about a granddaughter's health scare, ask for a report so you can pray.

If there's an upcoming important moment—surgery, medical report, job interview, big game, audition, graduation, move, or anything else that's important to the person—put it in your calendar and send a text on that day to say you're praying about it. Not long ago, a friend told me about his wife's cancer diagnosis and upcoming surgery. I put it in my calendar, and that morning when the surgery was scheduled, I let him know I was praying for her, for him, and for everyone in the family. (We'll look at this in more detail later.)

ENGAGE WITH THE KIDS

My dad was a pastor when I grew up, so I know what it's like to be ignored by people who want something from my dad. To them, I didn't even exist. In fact, some of them treated me the way the guy in the job interview treated Jenni and the boys—they didn't even look at me, even when I was standing next to my dad. But I also noticed that some people were very attentive to me … when my dad was nearby, but they totally ignored me when he wasn't. They were using their fake attention to gain leverage with my dad. When I was a kid, a man in the church asked if he could take me out for some ice cream. The whole time, he asked questions about my dad. He wanted to know if I'd heard him say anything about who he was going to hire for a particular position, and he asked if I knew anything about a project Dad was launching. At the time, I thought his questions were just odd, but later I realized he was trying to use me to get to my dad.

There's an inherent danger in using all the relational skills in this book: We can use them to honor people, or we can use them to manipulate them. Don't use fake interest in a person's spouse or kids to get them on your side! Paul wrote to the Romans, "Let love be without hypocrisy" (Romans 12:9). That means we love them, whether people respond the way we want them to or not.

Do you think people can discern our motives? Some can't, but many can. When they sense we're insincere in our interest, we've enflamed deep suspicion toward us. But when they know we're genuinely interested in them and their families, we connect on a much deeper level. That's certainly true for me. When people communicate that they care about Jenni and the boys, it touches my heart.

Value the spouse and children simply because your key influencers value them. Value them when they're with the key influencer and when they're not. If the Holy Spirit whispers to you that you're crossing the line into manipulation, confess it, trust God to forgive, and ask Him to show you more of His immeasurable love, so that's what flows out of you.

VALUE KIDS TO THEIR PARENTS

One of my favorite things to do is to brag on kids to their parents. I try to always find something I can highlight, even if it's something they said or did in the current conversation. It's amazing how a simple word of affirmation lifts spirits and gives people a sense of being seen and treasured. When we shine a spotlight on their children, parents beam. We're noticing greatness in the kids, and we're noticing greatness in the parents … in a role where they often feel insecure.

Not long ago, I was with Chris Railey at our church. His son Canon came over to say hello. I put my arm around him and said to Chris, "Guess what Canon did?"

Chris laughed, "What now? Whatever it is, I believe it!"

With my arm firmly around Canon, I told Chris, "He texted me Sunday afternoon to tell me how much he liked the message I'd preached that morning. He said he learned a lot. I wrote him back to let him know that meant a lot to me."

I then turned to Canon and said, "I'm not kidding. For you to take the time to be so thoughtful to encourage me like that … it's huge! It means more than you can know. In fact, it's the biggest encouragement

I got from anybody. Thank you, Canon. I'm sure you learned that from your dad because he's one of the most encouraging people I've ever known."

TELL THE KIDS HOW MUCH YOU RESPECT THEIR PARENTS

Another of my favorite things to do is to tell kids how much I think of their parents. I often ask parents if I can have a few minutes with their children, and I sit with them. I ask if they mind if I tell them something about their mom and dad. They're often a bit nervous to have a conversation with someone outside their circle of regular relationships, so I assure them I'm harmless, and it won't take long.

I describe the impact their parents have on other people, and I give a few specifics. I explain that God must think they're special to put them in such a wonderful family. I look at each child and say, "You probably already know this, but your dad is amazing. I appreciate him so much. And your mom is special ... but you know that. They mean so much to me. I'm so thankful for your mom and dad, and I'm so proud of you. I'm absolutely convinced that God has a terrific future for you. I see greatness in you." I then describe something I've seen or heard about them, and I asked them if they mind if I pray for them. I ask God's blessings on each child and the parents. (Sometimes, parents tell me their child has said, "Are we going to see that man who prayed for us? Who is he anyway?" And when I do Zoom calls with pastors I mentor, their children often want to interrupt to say, "Hi!" to me. (I love that.)

God uses these brief conversations to encourage the kids and build up the parents in their eyes, and they also convince the parents that I value their role in their kids' lives. It also gives me an opportunity to pray for the family.

I had the chance to meet with the three daughters of a couple who are leaders in our church. As I talked to them, I sensed that one of them was feeling insecure. I encouraged all of them, but I spent a few more minutes with her. I told her God had something special for her, and He would use every struggle to make her stronger. The next day, her mother called me to tell me how much those few minutes meant to her daughter. She explained, "She's been very depressed, and she had lost hope in her future. Your kind words have restored her hope. You can't know what that meant for her … and for her father and me. Thank you so much."

All I had done was notice her and take a couple of extra minutes to speak a few words of affirmation to her. But it mattered. It really mattered.

TOO, TOO, TOO

When I told a pastor about this principle, he smiled and jokingly asked, "But Scott, aren't you too busy to do all this?"

He knows me too well to think that the answer would be "Yes." I said, "Let me explain it this way: When I take some time to encourage kids, I'm making an investment in the kingdom of God because these kids will be the leaders of the future. But I'm also assuring the parents that they're not just spare parts in the ministry machine I'm running. I care about them, and I care about what they care about. When I take time to engage with their kids, it sends a powerful message about the heart of God, the heart of the church, and the heart of their pastor."

Then the pastor jokingly asked, "But Scott, aren't you too important to waste your time on kids?"

He knew to stand back for this one. I told him that was the opinion of the disciples when Jesus picked up the little children and loved them. I can almost hear them: "Kids? Why would anybody waste time on them? And certainly not You, Jesus! You've got better things to do!" The Scriptures say that Jesus was "indignant" when He heard them. He was angry because they had missed the heart of His message: No one is too insignificant. No one is too far gone. No one is beyond the reach of the love of Jesus.

"Yeah," the pastor smiled. "But isn't it too awkward for grown-ups to talk to kids?"

I admit that some of us lean away from engaging kids in conversation because we just don't know how. It feels uncomfortable because we're afraid we'll say something stupid and embarrassing. I understand. These are holy moments, and we need to be careful to avoid blowing it.

Don't try to be too cool. You're probably not going to compete with their favorite YouTuber or video game. Don't even try. Just be yourself. They know when you're trying to impress them—and they know how lame you look when you try and fail! Don't do it. And don't touch them. Today's culture isn't right for us to touch children. If they reach out to hug or touch you, that's fine, but don't initiate it. You may think I'm overreacting, but I'm not. Don't do anything to ruin the moment.

In your talks with kids, use the listening skills we examined a couple of chapters ago. Ask good questions, such as, "What do you like about school?" or "What do you enjoy doing?" and really listen. Use the golden statement: "Tell me more about that." And reflect what you hear them saying. It doesn't need to be a long conversation, but it should be meaningful.

I'LL NEVER FORGET

Troy and Lacey Hartman are the pastors of Rock Hills Church in Manhattan, Kansas, the home of Kansas State University. They have a great church and are amazing people. I got to know them through my son Dillon, who played football for KSU. Dillon will tell you that when he was in school, he struggled with all the distractions of being an athlete in a college environment. He was partying with friends, and he gradually drifted away from God and the church. At about the same time, Troy and Lacey and their two little girls, Jovi and Jade, planted a church in Manhattan, and I prayed that God would somehow work it out for Troy and Dillon to connect. God answered my prayers.

Troy became like an older brother to Dillon, and Lacey was like an older sister. Jovi and Jade loved Dillon like only little sisters can. The Hartman clan gave Dillon a home away from home. They invited him over for dinners, talked with him about anything and everything, and encouraged him in every way. They asked him to be on their launch team, and to my amazement, he said, "Yes!" A few months later, Dillon was on the set-up team and bringing several friends to church. When I saw his Instagram posts with pictures of big, strapping football players in church with him, tears of gratitude came to my eyes.

God used the love of Troy and Lacey to connect with Dillon and draw him back to a close relationship with the Lord. And today, Dillon is married to Holly, an incredible young woman. They're doing ministry in innovative ways to reach people who often fall outside the impact of the traditional church.

Jenni and I worried and prayed for Dillon when he was drifting, so when we see the Hartmans, our hearts explode with joy and gratitude. In fact, they'll never buy a meal when I'm around! When they call, I stop whatever I'm doing to answer the phone. Why? Because they loved my son and treated him like family when he needed someone to step into his life with grace and truth. They were the answer to one of the biggest prayers of my life, and I'll never forget them.

God is calling all of us, in one way or another, to play the role the Hartmans have played (and continue to play) in our family's journey to walk with God. They care about our son. When we care for the families of our key influencers, we build bonds that are deep and strong.

THINK ABOUT IT:

1) If you haven't already, enter family information in your contacts on your phone about each of your ten key influencers. Include the names of each family member, and important facts and dates.

2) This week, make it a point to engage the kids of at least two of your staff members or key influencers and use information about their families as a jumping off point for conversations.

3) Who is a leader you know who connects well with children? What can you learn from that person?

4) Do you use any of the excuses mentioned in this chapter to avoid engaging with kids (too busy, too important, or too awkward)? Explain your answer.

5) This week, carve out time to go to one event where a key influencer will be with his family (a ball game, a concert or recital, a play, etc.), and just enjoy being with them and showing support. Don't talk about church vision, strategy, or programs … and by all means, don't talk about church politics!

6) Offer to stay with a key influencer's kids, so the couple can have a night out.

7) Or invite the key influencer's whole family to have dinner with you and your family.

Chapter 11

10X MOMENTS

In August of 2019, I attended the biannual General Council for the Assemblies of God in Orlando, Florida. For the previous two years, my father had been suffering from Lewy Body Dementia, but his health was otherwise surprisingly good. I left home with no concern about his condition. On the night of August 2, several of us were taking a break from the conference by going to a movie. At 8:30 p.m., in the middle of the movie, my brother Bracy texted: "Dad's not doing well. Please call me." I got up and went to the lobby, so I could talk to him. He told me that Dad's condition was rapidly deteriorating, and he probably wouldn't last more than a few hours.

I was shocked. I couldn't believe it. I told him, "I was just there, and he was doing fine!"

Bracy explained, "Yeah, I know, but the doctor told us his body is shutting down. It's looking really bad, Scott." He let it sink in, and then he said, "I'm here with Dad. Why don't you FaceTime with him, so you can tell him goodbye."

My heart was racing and broken at the same time. Bracy held the phone, so I could see Dad, and through my tears, I told him, "I love you so much. You mean the world to me. I'll always remember what a great dad you are!"

Then Bracy got back on the call and said, "False alarm. He's doing better now."

What? Can this be happening? I stammered, "Okay. Okay. That's good. I'll talk to you tomorrow." We ended the call, and I went back to my seat.

One of the guys with me was my friend Anthony Scoma, one of the funniest people I know. He leaned over and whispered, "Hey, where have you been?"

I didn't want to interrupt the movie too much, so I just said, "It's my dad. He's dying."

At that moment in the movie, the main character, Rick Dalton, was feeling discouraged, so his best friend, Cliff Booth, yelled to him out of a car window as Rick was walking away, "Hey! You're *Rick effin' Dalton*, and don't you forget it!" Dalton was immediately encouraged. And the next moment, the electricity in the theater went out. We were sitting in the pitch-black dark, and Anthony spoke in the same dialect as Cliff Booth. He turned to me and said, "Hey, you're *Scott effin' Wilson,* and don't you forget it!"

We all laughed, but in the darkness, a guy said, "Oh, my gosh! You really are Scott Wilson! I read your book *Ready, Set, Grow* when I was in seminary. It's my favorite book we studied!" He was a pastor who was attending the General Council and was taking a break, too. We all laughed, first at Anthony and then with the pastor.

The power came back on, and the movie resumed. I settled in and tried to relax. A few minutes later, Bracy called back. I got up and ran to the lobby. I was having a hard enough time with the flood of emotions I'd experienced in the previous few minutes. What did he want to tell me now?

"Dad's gone, Scott. He's gone."

I wanted to ask a million questions, but all I could say was, "I'll get on the first flight."

Immediately, I contacted airlines, but the first flight with open seats was the next afternoon. I felt helpless.

My son Hunter was with me. When I told him about my dad, we stood in the lobby of the theater hugging each other. I had lost my father, and he had lost his grandfather. In the middle of his grief, he called two of my closest friends, Chris Railey and Justin Lathrop, who were also at the conference. By this time, the movie was over, and we went out the front doors to walk back to the hotel, but while we'd been inside, it had started raining hard. As we walked down the sidewalk, I saw Chris and Justin running toward us. They were drenched, but they didn't care. We hugged, and I told them what had just happened in the theater when Anthony mimicked the character in the film. We laughed, cried, laughed again, and cried a bit more. It was a special experience with them. To me, that's real love and true friendship.

I'll never forget how Hunter and my friends were there for me. And I'll always remember how Anthony interjected some humor. We'll always have that moment, that shared memory. All of us were close before that night, and we've done a lot together over the years, but that night cemented our love for each other. It was, to me at least, ten times (10x) more important than anything else we've done together.

BIGGER, DEEPER, STRONGER

Not all moments are the same. Some are more important than others, and a few are far more important. When we're there for people in these pivotal times, they'll never forget it. But the other side is just as true: If we're not there, they won't forget that either. Every key influencer has a few events and situations that are ten times more important than any others. Know this. Be there. It matters. These are 10x moments.

Some of these are happy and pleasant times, and we show up to join in the celebration. They include:

- ◆ Weddings.
- ◆ Graduations.
- ◆ Award presentations.
- ◆ Birthdays.
- ◆ Retirement parties.

It was, to me at least, ten times (10x) more important than anything else we've done together.

But others are like that night in the theater a thousand miles from home. They might be:

- ◆ Emergency calls from the ER.
- ◆ Major surgeries.
- ◆ A tragic diagnosis.
- ◆ Suicide.
- ◆ Overdose.
- ◆ Bankruptcy.
- ◆ Death from any cause.

One day I was hanging out with my family at home. I had put my phone on a table in another room, and a little while later when I picked it up, I saw that I'd missed a call from my friend Jonathan Pitts. I listened to the voicemail he had left me, and instantly, I knew something was terribly wrong. There was background noise, and he sounded frantic. He had just rushed his wife, Wynter, to the hospital, and it didn't look good. He told me she had said she wasn't feeling very well, so she went to their bedroom to rest. A few minutes later, he went in to check on her, but she was unresponsive. The doctors were trying to revive her, but she had passed away.

I ran to the car and sped to the hospital. I spent the rest of the evening and the next day with Jonathan. Jenni came, too. She and I stayed with him and his daughters. We didn't have to say anything profound. We were just there. We love Jonathan and his family, and we were (and still are) heartbroken over Wynter's death. I can't always be there for everybody like this, but I knew God had assigned Jenni and me to walk with Jonathan and his girls through the valley of the shadow of death.

Jonathan and I were good friends before that terrible day, but since then, our souls are inextricably connected. I love him like a brother, and Jenni and I would do anything for his girls.

When 10x moments happen, do everything you can to be there. If you can't be there in person, find some way to connect.

Call or FaceTime

Not long ago, my friend Shawn Thomas got some incredible news. His son Jared was going into his junior year in high school, and he had been offered a scholarship to play baseball at the University of Texas, one of the nation's premier programs. The kid is a stud. He's a left-handed pitcher and a very good hitter. From the time he was a little boy, Jared had dreamed of playing for the Longhorns at Disch-Falk Field in Austin.

I knew what Shawn was feeling at that moment because I remembered going crazy when Dillon got a scholarship to be a kicker for Kansas State. I wasn't there when Shawn found out, but I didn't want to miss out on the celebration. As soon as Jenni told me, I FaceTimed Shawn. He was at a coffee shop, so it wasn't appropriate for him to yell and cheer, so I did it for him. I started singing "The Eyes of Texas" and jumping around. (I'm sure the people sitting near Shawn could hear every word. He probably didn't tell them the screeching they heard was his pastor.) I said, "Get Jenni and me some tickets because we're going to see Jared play! We'll plan a road trip with y'all. Way to go, Shawn. You've raised a great and gifted son!"

Later, I heard from a number of people who said that Shawn had told them about my FaceTime call … how much it meant to him, and how many stares he'd gotten from people in the coffee shop. He told them he was touched that I'd celebrate with him like Jared was one of my sons.

It was my great pleasure to be there, if only on FaceTime, in Shawn's 10x moment.

Send or bring a gift

On the night Jenni and I were installed as global pastors at Oaks Church, I was amazed when I saw so many lead pastors from across the country sitting in the audience. Some had driven a long way, and some had flown in for the event. They came even in the middle of the COVID-19 pandemic just to be there with us. Many of them are pastors who consider me their spiritual father, so it was like having my extended family there.

It's amazing what a few lines in a text can mean to someone.

I invited them to come to our house after the ceremony. When they arrived, they had a surprise for Jenni and me: a Yeti cooler with a big wad of money in it! One of them was the spokesman. He told us, "That's for you to do something really fun." They gave me some monogrammed golf balls and hand towels to hang on my golf bag. The inscription on the balls read "Scott Wilson, Global Pastor, Spiritual Father, Multiplying Spiritual Fathers and Mothers." You could hardly see the ball under all that! And they gave Jenni a beautiful new purse with money inside for her to go shopping. They gathered around us and told us how much we meant to them, and they described the impact we've had on them. Tears filled my eyes, and tears are in my eyes right now as I think about their expressions of love for Jenni and me that night.

It was obvious they had carefully planned all this. Their thoughtfulness meant so much to us. They noticed what we like to do, they pitched in for the gifts, and they brought them to us at our 10x moment.

Special dates

Today, as I'm writing this, I got a text from our friends, Stony and Kim Halbrook. It reads, "We remembered this morning this is the one-year anniversary of your dad's passing. We wanted you to know that we remember, we're praying for you, and we love you. Your dad made a major impact on our lives and our family."

It's amazing what a few lines in a text can mean to someone. I cherish the fact that Stony and Kim care enough about me to write the date in their calendar, so they could remember it and reach out to encourage me when they knew it would be a hard day for me. This is a special 10x moment. Their kindness today reminds me that they came to Dad's funeral, and they've continued to love me, Jenni, our boys, and my mother throughout the year. What a gift they are to us.

When you put someone's 10x moment in your calendar and connect with them on that date, it compounds the impact of your love. It only takes a few seconds—on the original day and on the anniversary—but it has a priceless influence on those you love.

Turning regular moments into 10x ones

Someone asked me, "What's more important, quality time or quantity time with people?"

I responded, "Both!"

Sometimes, life is so hectic that it's easy to miss time with people we care about. If we've been too busy too long (and we can sense it, can't we?), we need to create a special time with them. For instance, my son Dakota and I love to go to concerts together. We make a point of going to one or two a year, and we can't wait for each one. Last year, we saw Willie Nelson at Billy Bob's in Fort Worth. The place was packed, and Willie did not disappoint! We were squashed together with thousands of people who all wanted to dance, but there was hardly enough room to wriggle. (This was, of course, before COVID-19.) It was a thoroughly memorable experience with Dakota, but it's not the only one.

A few years ago, we went to hear Alabama Shakes. It was open seating, so we got there early and waited in line for hours because Dakota wanted to be near the stage. We had the time of our lives, singing at the top of our lungs, dancing, and acting crazy together. I'll never forget that night, and I'm pretty sure he won't either. In fact, every time we drive to another concert, we relive the ones before, and we start making plans for the next one. As I write this, memories of concerts flood my mind and love for Dakota floods my heart. These are special 10x moments with him.

I've learned to look for ways to make everyday interactions into, well, if not 10x moments, at least 5X ones. When we have dinner together, I look for ways to make it special. Recently, when we watched a Beach Boys documentary, I paused the show several times to talk about what we were learning about the band and ask Dakota questions about them. He knows so much about music that he blows me away! I love spending time with him and our whole family. We can just hang out in the living room or the back porch and talk about amazing or crazy things that have happened to us. We love those times together.

I've found that the spontaneous moments make the planned times even more special. That's true for our families, and it's also true for our relationships with key influencers. That's how stronger, deeper relationships develop.

Quality or quantity? Yes, both.

CREATING 10X MOMENTS

You don't have to wait for a phone call to have special times with your key influencers. You can create them, but you have to be intentional. They don't just happen, and they aren't limited to weddings, funerals, and birthdays. Here are some suggestions:

Trips

There's nothing like getting people away from their normal routines and pressures. Ken Marks is one of the most influential people in our church, an incredible man of God. A decade ago, I wanted to find a way to build a stronger relationship with him, and God gave me a great idea: I would take him on a trip to Belarus in Eastern Europe to help me teach a group of pastors and business leaders. He agreed to go, and it was fantastic! Just recently, he sent me a text: "Scott, do you remember when we went to Belarus? That trip changed my life.

Thanks for taking me with you!" He was saying, "Thanks for creating a 10x moment with me."

By the way, Ken loved going to Belarus with me so much that he went six times in three years. Each time, he took off work and endured 20-hour flights there and back. Why? Because they were 10x moments that changed his life and connected the two of us in such a special way that we'll have that bond forever.

Retreats

Robin Kelly is the owner of a very successful construction company. He stays incredibly busy, so I was very excited when he accepted my invitation to join eight select guys and me on a retreat. On the way to the hunting lodge where we planned to do very manly things—shooting, golfing, and eating massive amounts of meat—we stopped at a barbecue joint. When we got our plates and sat down, Robin said, "Pastor, I know you've been dealing with your dad's Alzheimer's."

"Yes," I responded. "It's been rough."

He leaned in. "Well, at least you had a dad. Mine died when I was five. I never had anyone to play catch with, to teach me how to shave, tie a tie, or ride a bike. At least you had that."

I could feel the pain in his voice, and he had opened the door to the rest of the guys to talk about their relationships with their fathers. And so we did, for the next three hours. The men shared a lot of pain.

As we got up from the table and walked out into the parking lot to get in the SUVs, the men spontaneously stopped and hugged, assuring each other that it's going to be okay. It was amazing. We hadn't even gotten to the lodge, but God had already given us a 10x moment.

Honor

To make new board members or staff members at our church feel valued, we conduct a "sword ceremony" for each installation. At their first meeting, I call them to come forward, and I hand them a sword inscribed with their name, the year, and the words "All Together." Before I hand it to them, I tell the story of King Arthur and the Knights of the Round Table. They always brought their swords and laid them down on the table, symbolizing their commitment to bring their influence, their wealth, their talents, and their lives to serve the kingdom of Camelot.

Then I say, "We're serving a King who is greater than all kings, the King of the entire universe. We've been invited to sit at His table. Ours isn't round. It's rectangular, and He sits at its head. We submit everything we have, everything we do, and everything we are to our King. We commit to follow His will and His directions. I'm asking you to come to every meeting with this attitude, to lay everything down for our King, saying, 'I give everything for the sake of the Kingdom of God.' If this is your commitment, say, 'Yes, this is my commitment.'"

I then pray over them. I can't remember a time when there weren't tears and sincere emotions expressed. When I go to their homes or offices, I see those swords hanging proudly (or maybe I should say humbly) on a wall in a prominent place.

You can probably think of other ways to create 10x moments with your key influencers, but my guess is that if you aren't doing it with your family, you probably aren't doing it with the key leaders around you. Start wherever you are. Respond to the ones that are obvious, create ones that are special, and trust God to use all of them to build much stronger connections with the people you love and lead.

THINK ABOUT IT:

1) What were two or three crucial moments in your life when someone was there for you? How did that person's presence affect you?

2) Has there been a time when no one showed up for a tragedy in your life or your family? How did their absence affect you?

3) Think about your key influencers, and write a plan for how you'll:

   ◆ Call or FaceTime to connect with them

   ◆ Send or bring gifts to show appreciation

   ◆ Record special dates to remember and show you care

- Turn normal times into special times

4) How have you created 10x (or maybe 5x) moments in the past?

5) What are some possible 10x moments you can plan for the next six months to a year? What difference will they make?

Chapter 12

NO STRINGS ATTACHED

We live in a "reciprocal society." That means almost every interaction is transactional: I'll do this for you, but only if you'll do that for me. To be fair, that's how capitalism operates, and our economy would collapse without it. But God's approach to us is gracious, not transactional. He loved us when we were His enemies, when we had absolutely nothing to offer Him, when it cost Jesus His life to rescue us. The "one another" passages in the New Testament are based on the principle that we can only love, forgive, accept, and encourage others to the extent we've experienced the love, forgiveness, acceptance, and encouragement from God.

As a preamble to the beautiful poem about Christ in Philippians, Paul says our relationships with each other are the result of our experience of God's amazing grace:

Therefore if you have any encouragement from being united with Christ, if any comfort from his love, if any common sharing in the Spirit, if any tenderness and compassion, then make my joy complete by being like-minded, having the same love, being one in spirit and of one mind. Do nothing out of selfish ambition or vain conceit. Rather, in humility value others above yourselves, not looking to your own interests but each of you to the interests of the others.

In your relationships with one another, have the same mindset as Christ Jesus ... —Philippians 2:1-5

When the river of life—the experience of Christ's encouragement, comfort, tenderness, and compassion—flows into us, it flows out of us into the lives of people around us. We begin to treat them the way God treats us—He loves us with incomprehensible joy and generosity! And we can then love others with no strings attached.

When I think about my relationships with my key influencers, I ask myself, *What do these people get that they wouldn't have gotten because they're on my team? What's the benefit to them, the upside that probably can't be measured but is very real?*

I know what it feels like for people to try to pull strings when they relate to me.

STRINGS ON ME

Earlier, I described instances when I was boy and my dad was the pastor, some men were very kind and attentive to me, but only because they wanted some inside scoop they couldn't get from my father.

Over the years, people have asked to see me, taken me to lunch, and given me gifts, but sooner or later, "the ask" for money or other resources caused me to realize they cared more about what I could do for them than about me.

In denominational politics, the deals cut are much like the ones in Washington. That's not a body slam; it's just the way things work. Like two congressmen voting for each other's bill, we lobby each other to vote for our agenda item.

Occasionally, I've been shocked by comments from people in our church. They've given a lot of money to a building campaign or a project, and when I thank them, they say something like, "So, are you putting me on the board now?"

I react, "Excuse me. I'm not sure what you're saying."

The answer comes back, "Well, Pastor, how much money do you have to give around here to get on the board?"

There are several things I'd like to say at that point, but I try to limit it to "That's not how it works. Positions on the board aren't up for sale."

Years ago, a man in our church regularly bought me expensive gifts. I didn't ask for them, and I didn't want them, but they showed up at my front door or my office. After each gift, he called to ask me to spend an afternoon with him or carve out a long lunch with him. At first, I accepted his invitation because I thought, *What could it hurt? I want to get to know the people in our church, and this guy is really trying to honor me.* In our conversations, when I mentioned a book I wanted to read, he'd jump in, "I'll buy it for you." Or if I said Jenni and I wanted to see a movie, he offered to buy the tickets.

I soon realized something wasn't right. These weren't actually gifts; they all had strings attached. The most obvious display that his approach to me was manipulative was his resentment any time I had to say, "I'm sorry. I can't make it. I'm really busy." He was sure his gifts had bought my friendship. A good friend asked me how I felt in that relationship, and I said, "Like a prostitute. He was trying to buy my time and friendship." Too harsh? Maybe, but that's how I felt.

Please don't generalize this too broadly. Don't assume that everyone who is nice to you is trying to manipulate you, but on the other hand, don't be surprised when you realize it's true. We talk often about experiencing the love of God, but authentic love for each other is too rare ... which makes it very precious. When you find it, treasure it. When you express it, watch how people respond.

ADDING VALUE

The way I can build genuine "one another" relationships with my key influencers is to add value to their lives as often as possible. When I'm with them, my only agenda is to help them become everything God wants them to be. I'm sure life on farms a hundred years ago was stressful, but at least there was time and space to think. Today, we live in an incredibly hectic, pressure-packed world with constant images of the perfect life, which leads to disappointment that we're experiencing something less. Our key influencers are neck deep in this cauldron of off-the-charts expectations. Everywhere they go, every person they see, every event in their lives drains their emotional, physical, and spiritual reserves. The last thing they need is to be around a pastor who drains them even more!

We talk often about experiencing the love of God, but authentic love for each other is too rare ... which makes it very precious.

I get about 50 asks a week: for money, speaking, positions, time, or another resource. Sometimes, people are really upset when I don't give them the answer they want to hear. My key influencers serve in important positions in their fields and probably get more asks than I do. I don't want them to assume I'm another ask in their week.

When the key influencers in our church think of me, I don't want them to cringe, roll their eyes, or walk the other way because they think I'm always asking them to contribute to my success. I want them to see me as life-giving—not life-draining. I want them to look forward to seeing me, to know I value them, and to never ever feel I value them only when they move my agenda forward. That's the kind of leader I want to be, and that's the kind of leader who builds close relationships, creating a culture of encouragement and celebration … with no strings attached. I want them to think, *That guy is always looking for ways to add to my life. He's a breath of fresh air. I love being with him!*

How do we add value to them? I'm glad you asked. Here are some recommendations:

Take them with you

When I go on missions trips overseas, I always invite one or two of the key influencers to go along. When I speak at an event, I take one of them with me. When I go to a conference, I invite one to join me. I want to give them experiences they probably wouldn't have any other way.

Make introductions

When I'm talking with people, they sometimes say, "Man, I wish I could meet so-and-so."

If I know the person, I say, "I know him. I can make the introduction right now." I pull out my phone, make the call, and introduce them so they can talk in more detail later. If the person isn't available, I leave a message and ask him to call me back.

I want key influencers to meet the incredible people I know. I've become friends with phenomenally gifted people over the years, and when I can connect a key influencer with one of these friends, it's a great pleasure. Sometimes, one of my key influencers needs expertise in a specific area, and I'm happy to put him in touch with a professional I've known and done business with. Actually, one of the things I enjoy most is being a switchboard to connect people.

Open doors

The introductions aren't only to tap into another person's talents. Sometimes, it's to open doors of opportunity for the key influencer, or more likely, one of their children who wants a career in a certain field where I know someone. When I can open a door like this, I know God is using me to play a significant role in that person's future. And I love it!

Give them your heart

One of the most important gifts you can give is yourself. When I'm giving myself to these key influencers, I'm going beyond the minimum. When I read a book that I think one of them would like, I buy a copy and give it to him, and I put a book mark in the places where I've marked paragraphs or pages that are most powerful to me. When Jenni and I enjoy a restaurant, we often take influential couples there the next time we go so we can share it together. When I go on a trip, I bring back gifts for the people on our board to show my appreciation for their support and prayers. Some of us are instinctively sensitive and generous, but like every other principle we've examined in this book, all of us can learn to do it. For instance, you might have a line item on your weekly planning sheet that says, "What is one special thing I can do for a key influencer this week?" Then do it.

Create Systems

I love people a lot, and I love a lot of people. To love them well, I have to create systems to help me connect with them and stay connected. Systems enable me to focus. I can easily spend too much time on this project or that responsibility, and when that happens, something (or someone) inevitably slips through the cracks.

You may have a very different strategy than the one I use, but to provide a jumping-off point, let me share a few ideas:

Notes of encouragement

Every week, a volunteer coordinator gives me a list of 15 volunteers who have done an outstanding job or need encouragement. I get the list every Tuesday, and I send each one a handwritten note. The list from the coordinator has their names, a picture if she has one, and a paragraph describing what she thinks I might say. With the list, she gives me 15 note cards. When I'm finished, she makes sure the notes get in the mail that day. This practice lets me say "Thank you!" to people who are working hard but who may never show up on my radar because they're working behind the scenes in roles that don't normally intersect with mine.

Do you think the volunteer coordinator sees this responsibility as a hassle and wasted time? No way. She often tells me how delighted people have been when they read the card, and they're more motivated than ever to serve.

Sometimes, when I visit someone's home, I see one of my cards on a mirror or the refrigerator. That tells me all I need to know about the impact of those few minutes of care for them.

Prayer texts

Every morning, I look at my calendar. At the top is a tab that says "Add Value." When I click on it, I see the name of one of the seven people in my immediate family and one of the key influencers. I start my day praying for those two people, and I send a text saying something like, "I'm praying for you this morning. I'm trusting that God will give you the strength, wisdom, and encouragement you need to face everything in your world today. I thank God for you, and I want you to know how much I appreciate all you do for Him. I love you. Have a great day!" Of course, these people are always on my mind and in my heart, so I almost always know of something specific to mention about their situations when I send the text.

Before, during, and after

When I have an appointment to meet with a key influencer, I don't just show up and hope things go well. I almost always send an agenda 24 hours before we meet to give a heads up about what I want to talk about. Then, when we meet, I take notes to make sure I don't forget anything important. I write down the action items we've decided to pursue, along with a timeline and due dates. I send these notes to the person that day or the next day.

Before I started doing this, there was "entropy" after these meetings. Entropy is "a tendency toward randomness." In other words, ideas become confused and decisions fade away. Preparation and thoroughness take only a few minutes, and they prevent a ton of headaches.

This habit is much more than a means of accountability for the leader and me; it's an encouragement tool. When I send the summary notes, I always affirm the person's heart and skills. I highlight the points in our discussion in which he was particularly insightful. I tell him I'm looking forward to our next time together. In this way, we're not just getting tasks accomplished; I'm adding value to his life every time we meet.

Never show up empty-handed

When Jenni and I go to someone's house, she makes sure we have a gift—and not just any gift, but a thoughtful one—for the person or couple we're visiting. And when we have people over to our house, we think about what those people enjoy and find a gift that will be, we hope, meaningful.

Recently, Justin and Andrea Lathrop moved back to our church. They had been living in Florida for the past few years, and we missed them a lot. When they got back, some people assumed they were glad to leave Florida and thrilled to be in Texas again, but it's a bit more complicated than that. As a housewarming gift, Jenni ordered a pillow with all the tourist attractions in Palm Beach illustrated on it and a Palm Beach dish towel. When Jenni gave them to Andrea, she told her, "I wanted to give you something to remind you of the good times you had in Florida and your special friends there."

Tears came to Andrea's eyes. She told Jenni, "Other people have told me to forget about all the wonderful people I got to know over the past six years, but you understand that these friendships mean a lot to me. You're so thoughtful."

This practice is second nature to Jenni because it's her love language, but I've learned to be more intentional about it. It takes a few minutes, and we save time by thinking ahead and ordering something to be delivered before the date, but it doesn't cost much to show you were thinking of them.

HOW CAN YOU TELL?

How can I know if people see me as a "value add guy" or a leach who is sucking them dry? It's not that hard to tell. I want to be the first person they call when they have a problem, and I want to be the first person they call when something spectacular happens, and they just want to tell somebody about it.

The men and women on our board know when they call, I'll answer if there's any way humanly possible. When a family member is in an accident, they call, and I go to be with them. When they're struggling in a relationship, they call to get advice.

Just last week (as I write this) a pastor I mentor called to tell me about a lady in his community who gave almost a million dollars to his church. He told me all about it, and he talked about how God could use that money to grow the church and reach far more people. Then he said, "Scott, I couldn't wait to call you. You're the first person I thought about calling because I knew you'd be as excited as me … well, *almost* as excited as me!"

IN YOUR COURT

I've given you a glimpse into my heart, and I've explained that my leadership strategy is based on two pillars: respect and relationship. I'm certainly not saying mine are the only five ways to earn respect, or you're limited to these five ways to build stronger relationships. You may have far better and far more ideas than I've had. That's fantastic! Use this book as a launch pad. Read other books to get better suggestions, talk to gifted leaders to discover their secrets, and trust God to give you a clear path to lead your key people well. I've given you my best shot. Now the ball is in your court.

In this book, you've read about dozens of ideas and recommendations, but don't try to do them all at once. Start by identifying one action point in each chapter (or even fewer if that's too much), put them into your agenda each week, and make them a priority. Some will come naturally, but some will require tenacity. Determine which ones have the biggest payoff, and make sure those become an integral part of your life and your connections with your key influencers.

In the opening story in the first chapter, I described my list of misguided motives to be seen as strong, gifted, and a great leader. But the Lord asked, "Where's love on your list?" I crossed out all those desires and wrote one word on my paper: Love. Experiencing the love of God, and out of that deep well, drawing out love to share with those around us. Building leaders to advance God's kingdom has one foundation, one message, one heart, and one banner: Jesus told us, "Love one another. As I have loved you, so you must love one another. By this everyone will know that you are my disciples, if you love one another" (John 13:34-35). That's what influence is all about.

THINK ABOUT IT:

1) What are some ways you can tell that someone has an ulterior motive for being nice to you?

   ◆ When that happens, how do you normally respond?

2) What do you think it means to "love with no strings attached"?

   ◆ Is it even possible? Why or why not?

3) The chapter lists several ways you can add value to the lives of your key influencers. Which ones do you need to work on? What will be some benefits?

4) The chapter also lists some systems to stay connected to people. Which of these will help you the most? When and how will you implement them?

5) Look back through the book. Identify one principle or practice you want to apply from each chapter. Write a plan about how you'll make them part of your regular schedule.

6) What is the single most important lesson you've learned from this book? What difference will it make in your relationships with key influencers?

ACKNOWLEDGMENTS

I'm so thankful for my close friend, Pat Springle, for helping me create this book. Thank you for helping me get my words in print. I am always amazed—but never surprised—at how each book comes together.

Thanks to Luke Brugger and Don Gibson for spending two days with me to go through all the material and helping me organize all my thoughts for this book. I have so much love and respect for both of you.

Thanks to The Father's Initiative and the Ready Set Grow team members for all the work they do to help pastors and leaders.

As always, I want to thank my wife and my best friend, Jenni. You are so good to me. I can't imagine doing life without you. I love you with all my heart. You have made such a difference in my life. Outside of Jesus, you have been the greatest example of love I've ever known. Every chapter of this book is filled with stories of how you have taught me to love. Thank you, Babe.

ABOUT THE AUTHOR

Scott Wilson is the global pastor of Oaks Church, ministering to approximately 4,000 people every week in the South Dallas area. He is a frequent conference speaker and provides mentorship for hundreds of pastors and church leaders.

He serves as the founder and director of The Father Initiative, an innovative organization that multiplies spiritual fathers and mothers for Kingdom transformation through church planting. The Father Initiative partners with other organizations involved in the church planting process to provide a family dynamic so that no church planter plants alone. For more information, go to fatherinitiative.com.

With more than 20 years of experience in full-time pastoral ministry, dozens of pastors and leaders have been strengthened to fulfill their destiny and dreams through Scott Wilson Consulting.

The organization comes alongside church and marketplace leaders to enable them to achieve the full potential of what God has called them to do.

Because of Scott's desire to train the next generation, he created the Oaks School of Leadership, a specialized ministry training program providing young leaders with hands-on experience while earning college credits. Through this intense training program, hundreds of students have been educated, prepared for ministry, and sent out as ministry leaders.

Scott has written several books, including his latest releases:

- *Identity: Discover Your Identity—The Search that Leads to Significance and True Success,*
- *Parenting with Purpose: 7 Keys to Raising Up World-Changers,*
- *P3: Praying in the Spirit, with Understanding, and in Agreement,*
- *Spread the Fire: Spirit Baptism in Today's Culture, and*
- *Clear the Stage: Making Room for God.*

Scott's previous titles include *The Next Level: A Message of Hope for Hard Times* (Baxter Press) and *Steering Through Chaos: Mapping a Clear Direction in the Midst of Transition and Change* (Zondervan).

ABOUT THE FATHER INITIATIVE

The Father Initiative

EVERY PASTOR NEEDS A SPIRITUAL FATHER

The Father Initiative multiplies spiritual fathers and mothers to multiply churches. The Apostle Paul said, "You have many teachers, but you don't have many fathers." We think that is just as true today as it was when it was written. It's time to do something about it. The missing component of our church multiplication models today is the presence of spiritual fathers and mothers, experienced pastors who carry the heart of the Father and are committed to the long-term success of the next generation of church leaders. While institutional support is helpful, there is no substitute for the enduring, relational investment of healthy, seasoned pastors. Time after time, we have heard from church planters and young pastors that they feel alone and ill-equipped, desperate not only for the relationships that a mentor and peer group could provide, but also for the wisdom of a leader who has navigated the personal, family, and organizational challenges they face. For the Church to be effective in the future, we must create solutions to not only raise up its next leaders from our congregations today, but we must also provide models to leverage the untapped wisdom and relational capacity of healthy, seasoned pastors. By 2030, we believe the Lord has given us a plan to raise up 1,000 spiritual fathers and mothers and plant over 4,000 churches together.

> "My wife Christina and I planted Overflow City Church near Washington, D.C., in the fall of 2018. Having a spiritual father to help us through this process has been a game-changer. Without one, the journey would have been much more challenging, and I feel like we wouldn't have had the tools and resources we needed. He has had a significant impact on our personal growth and the growth of our team. It's so great to know we are not alone in this"

> —Paul and Christina Hanfere
> Overflow City Church

For more information, go to fatherinitiative.com

INNER CIRCLE

A customized coaching journey to help you grow your church
There's a weight that comes with being a pastor. It feels intense because you know what's on the line—hundreds if not thousands of souls hanging in the balance. Knowing what you and your church do next will affect their eternity.

A lot of pastors are just trying to survive and get through the week. They feel scattered. Struggling to focus. Starting to doubt that they've got what it takes to lead.

You're not alone. We've been where you are now, and we've made it to the other side.

The Inner Circle is a three-year customized coaching journey that gives you everything you need to know and do to grow a church and become a high-performing pastor.

On this 36-month journey, you will be part of an exclusive group of high-performing pastors coached by Scott Wilson and his own elite growth team to consistently **discover** the next mountain to take, **design** the plan to get there, and **deliver** results you need to grow your church.

Deliverables: What You Get When You Join The Inner Circle

- Kickoff Retreat
- Activator Certification in *Intentional Growth Planning* System
- Comprehensive Resources Suite
- Monthly Group Cohort Calls
- Quarterly Results Assessments
- Lead Pastor dashboard to stay focused on High ROI Activities
- Church domain dashboard to stay focused on the 10 Church Essentials for Growth
- Personal access to our Inner Circle Team of Experts
- Duplicatable Strategic Growth Planning System
- Your own **Personal Success Guide**

Inner Circle Success Guides have comprehensive ministry experience and background. They are highly proficient in Inner Circle's coaching, application and assessment framework. This combination ensures a successful Inner Circle journey for you and your church.

To apply for the Inner Circle, go to readysetgrowchurch.com.

RESOURCES

PARENTING WITH PURPOSE:
7 KEYS TO RAISING UP WORLD-CHANGERS

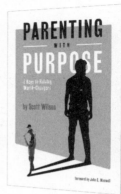

God has given us the most sweeping vision the world has ever known—to make disciples of people in every nation on earth and make a dierence wherever we go. And He has entrusted us with the people we need to equip to fulfill that vision—our children and grandchildren. The stakes couldn't be higher, and our role couldn't be more important. In this book, Pastor Scott Wilson encourages us to have a God-sized dream for our impact on the next generation, a dream that's far bigger than we can accomplish on our own, so we need to trust God more than ever . . . and a dream that reaches into generations to come. With warmth, humor, biblical teaching, and practical insights, this book equips all of us—par-ents, grandparents, teachers, coaches, and mentors—to instill God's heart into the children in our lives. That's His plan, and we are His strategy.

P3: PRAYING...IN THE SPIRIT, WITH UNDERSTANDING, AND IN AGREEMENT

In this book, Pastor Scott Wilson explains how God led him and his church to experience far more of His mind, His heart, and His direction than ever before. And it's not a secret. Church staff teams, small groups, couples, families, and congregations can tap more deeply into the presence of the Spirit. Pastor Scott tells the story about how God led him to the concepts of "P3 prayer," the biblical foundation of it, and the powerful process that enables all of us to listen as God speaks and "be filled with all the fulness of God." Do you want God to revolutionize your prayer life?

CLAIM YOUR FREE
ANNUAL SUBSCRIPTION

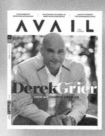

AT AVAILJOURNAL.COM
($59 VALUE)

AVAIL LEADERSHIP PODCAST

WITH VIRGIL SIERRA

FOLLOW
THE
LEADER

STAY CONNECTED